THE DIPLOMACY OF
GERMAN UNIFICATION

Also by Stephen F. Szabo

The Bundeswehr and Western Security (*editor*)

The Changing Politics of German Security

The Successor Generation:
International Perspectives of Postwar Europeans (*editor*)

THE DIPLOMACY OF GERMAN UNIFICATION

Stephen F. Szabo

St. Martin's Press
New York

Dedicated to Christine and Meg

First published in the United States of America 1992

Printed in the United States of America

ISBN 0-312-08057-3

Library of Congress Cataloging-in-Publication Data

Szabo, Stephen F.
The diplomacy of German unification / Stephen F. Szabo.
     p. cm.
    Includes bibliographical references (p.) and index.
    ISBN 0-312-08057-3
    1. Germany—History—Unification, 1990. 2. World politics—1985-1995.
    I. Title.
DD290.25.S93 1992
327'.0943—dc20   92-17119
                                           CIP

CONTENTS

PREFACE

This is a study in contemporary history, a discipline that the journalist Don Oberdorfer has described as the "first draft of history." It is an attempt to compile what is known about an event in the immediate wake of its occurrence (i.e., within two years of the conclusion of the treaty on Germany unity). While fuller studies will emerge later when documents have been declassified and events can be placed in a larger historical perspective, the advantage to an early study is that it captures the thoughts of the participants in a historical event while their memories are still fresh. It also provides a collection of contemporary materials to which future historians can refer.

This history is based on a number of types of sources. First is the journalistic and archival records of the events. Second are a few memoirs by people who were closely involved that already have appeared, most notably those of Horst Teltschik, the National Security Advisor to Chancellor Helmut Kohl during this period. Third are the interviews conducted for this book by the author. Key officials involved in the diplomacy of German unification in West and East Germany, the United States and the Soviet Union were interviewed, in almost all cases within a year of the signing of the final agreement in September 1990. These interviews were kept confidential in order to elicit as unvarnished an account of what occurred as possible. While interviews can often be self-serving and, like memoirs, offer perspectives limited by personal contacts and bureaucratic vantage points, they are especially important in this case because so much of the diplomacy was conducted informally and on a personal level.

The paper trail in this story will not be extensive simply because so much was done through face-to-face conversations and on the telephone. In addition, only a small group of people (probably less than thirty in all) was closely involved in the unification negotiations. But when the interviews are triangulated with the journalistic record and with events a rich picture emerges.

As in any major research effort, acknowledgement of the help of others is incumbent upon the author. The research assistance of Andrew Denison and Steven Sokol, graduate students at the Paul H. Nitze School of Advanced International Studies, Johns Hopkins University, was indispensable to the final product. They both did much digging for sources and interpretations and offered excellent insights and criticism. In addition the comments and suggestions of David Calleo, my colleague at the Nitze School, were, as always, invaluable, as was the support and encouragement of the school's dean, George Packard. The collaboration of R. G. Livingston and the American Institute for Contemporary German Studies, Johns Hopkins University, in the co-sponsorship with the Nitze School of a seminar series entitled "The Diplomacy of German Unity" was an important source of inspiration and information. Thanks as well to Catherine Kelleher and Wolfram Hanrieder, who read earlier versions of the text, and to Ms. Mary Elizabeth Glover and Ms. Kim Neale who helped with the preparation of the manuscript. As always, the final result is the full responsibility of the author.

A final word of appreciation to my wife Joan and to my daughters, Meg and Christine, who provided moral support and inspiration for this effort. This book is dedicated to our daughters, who will grow up with the new Germany.

Chronology of the Diplomacy of German Unification

1989

30 May	George Bush calls the Federal Republic a "partner in leadership" on his visit to the FRG following the NATO Summit.
12-15 June	Helmut Kohl meets with Mikhail Gorbachev in Bonn.
27 June	Erich Honecker meets with Gorbachev in Moscow.
19 August	Seven hundred East German citizens flee to Austria via Hungary.
11 September	Hungary opens border to Austria for East Germans.
12 September	New Forum, the major East German opposition group, is founded.
30 September	Hans-Dietrich Genscher visits Prague. Six thousand East German refugees at the West German embassy there are granted permission to travel to the FRG.
1 October	First trains with East German refugees from West German embassies in Prague and Warsaw enter the FRG.
2 October	First mass demonstrations in Leipzig.
7 October	Gorbachev visit to East Berlin to celebrate the fortieth anniversary of the GDR. Large demonstrations take place, and Gorbachev states his memorable phrase: "He who comes late, life will perish."
9 October	Over 100,000 people on the streets of Leipzig and other cities demonstrate for "freedom of speech and reforms." The decision is made not to use force.
18 October	Honecker resigns. Egon Krenz becomes the new General Secretary.

1 November	Krenz meets with Gorbachev in Moscow.
9 November	Günter Schabowski, press spokesman of the Communist Party (SED), announces a new visa procedure that is interpreted as meaning that the Berlin Wall is open. A rush of East Germans into West Berlin in effect opens the Wall.
13 November	Hans Modrow is elected Minister President.
17 November	Modrow makes a government statement in which he discusses a "community of treaties" (*Vertragsgemeinschaft*) between the two Germanies.
28 November	Kohl presents to the Bundestag his Ten Point Plan for German unity, which proposes creating "confederative structures" with the goal of establishing a "federation."
2/3 December	Bush-Gorbachev summit at Malta. Ongoing situation in Germany is a central discussion topic.
3 December	Krenz, the SED Politburo, and Central Committee all resign.
4 December	Brussels. Bush meets with Kohl. He assures U.S. support for unification and urges adherence to four principles: 1) that self-determination be respected; 2) that unification be part of a broader process of European integration through NATO and the EC; 3) that unification be gradual and peaceful; and 4) that the inviolability of borders be respected as stated in the Helsinki Final Act. Subsequently, Bush briefs NATO allies, claiming U.S. support of unification in the "context of continued commitment to NATO [and] an increasingly integrated European Community."
6 December	François Mitterrand visits Kiev with Gorbachev and reportedly asks Gorbachev to prevent German unification.
7 December	Roundtable discussions begin in East Berlin. Elections set for May 6, 1990.
10 December	Four Power meeting in Berlin initiated by the Soviets.

12 December	James Baker III gives speech in Berlin. He visits Modrow in Potsdam.
15 December	Lothar de Maizière becomes head of East German CDU.
17 December	Gregor Gysi becomes new head of renamed Communist Party.
18 December	Kohl meets with Modrow in Dresden.
21 December	Mitterrand meets Modrow in East Berlin.
22 December	Brandenburg Gate is opened.

1990

3 January	Soviet war memorials defaced. Conflict over restoration of Stasi as "constitutional protection force."
8 January	Roundtable of opposition groups protests the restoration of the Stasi.
15 January	Demonstrations take place. East Berlin Stasi headquarters occupied. Concern over potential violence increases. Modrow government gives in.
28 January	Elections moved up to March 18 in response to erosion of Modrow government's power. Modrow agrees with the roundtable to form a "government of national responsibility."
29 January	British Foreign Secretary Douglas Hurd discusses the 2 + 4 proposal in Washington.
30 January	Modrow meets Gorbachev in Moscow. Gorbachev says that the Soviet Union does not "in principle" object to unification.
31 January	The Genscher Plan is presented at the Tutzung Protestant Academy.
1 February	Modrow presents a plan (*"Deutschland, einig Vaterland"*) laying out a step-by-step process to achieve German unification.

2 February	Genscher visits Washington and receives support for the Genscher Plan and CSCE summit. Baker proposes the 2 + 4 framework.
8 February	Baker proposes 2 + 4 in Moscow, having discussed it with French Foreign Minister Roland Dumas on a stopover en route.
10 February	Kohl and Genscher in Moscow where they obtain the "key to German unity." Gorbachev says the question of unity must be decided by the German people.
12 February	Ottawa "Open Skies" summit. The Foreign Ministers of the two German states and the Four Powers agree to begin formal talks on German unity under the 2 + 4 framework.
14 February	Modrow visits Bonn. His request for DM 15 billion in aid is rejected. Bonn talks of economic and monetary union.
15 February	Kohl and Mitterrand meet in Paris.
24-25 February	Kohl and Bush meet at Camp David.
Early March	Conflict between Genscher and Kohl regarding the Polish border comes to a head, with intimations of a coalition breakup. Kohl gives in, and both German parliaments will unconditionally guarantee current borders.
8 March	President Wojciech Jaruzelski of Poland visits Paris.
14 March	Initial meeting of 2 + 4 parties at the ambassadorial level. Agreement that Polish representatives should be present when issues affecting them are discussed.
18 March	Elections in the five eastern *Länder* (states) won by the CDU with 48.2 percent of the vote. SPD had 21.8 percent, Liberals 5.3 percent, PDS 16.3 percent, Bündnis 90, 2.9 percent.
12 April	Coalition formed in the GDR. De Maizière is elected Prime Minister of the GDR.

19 April   Kohl and Mitterrand propose European political and monetary union by 1993.

5 May   Bonn 2 + 4 meeting. Poles to participate in July session. Soviets offer to "decouple" domestic developments from agreements on external aspects.

14 May   Secret meeting between Horst Teltschik and Gorbachev. German financial support offered to feed and house and then move Soviet troops out of the GDR.

15 May   Kohl calls for all-German elections by the end of the year.

31 May   Washington summit. "Nine Assurances" offered to Gorbachev, generally implying that the United States and NATO will not use unification to take advantage of the Soviet Union.

8 June   Kohl meets with Bush at Camp David.

21 June   Parliaments of both German states pass resolutions recognizing Poland's western border as final and call for a treaty between Poland and Germany following unification.

22 June   East Berlin 2 + 4 meeting.

1 July   Economic and currency union established.

2 July   Twenty-eighth Soviet Communist Party (CPSU) Congress begins in Moscow.

3 July   Speech by Eduard Shevardnadze at the Party Conference in favor of German unification.

4 July   Meeting between Kohl, Genscher and Gerhard Stoltenberg. Decision reached to limit Bundeswehr strength to 370,000.

5 July   NATO summit in London. Atlantic Alliance mission is redefined, and the unilateral limit on the size of the Bundeswehr is accepted.

9-12 July	Houston economic summit of G-7 leaders. Kohl and Mitterrand fail to obtain agreement on $15 billion Western aid package to the Soviet Union.
15-16 July	Gorbachev and Kohl meet near Stavropol. German NATO membership accepted by Gorbachev. In return, Kohl pledges to limit German armed forces to 370,000, pay DM 12 billion to facilitate the withdrawal of the Red Army within four years, provide wide-ranging economic and technical assistance to the Soviet Union and sign a friendship treaty.
17 July	Paris 2 + 4 meeting. Agreement on Polish border reached.
3 August	Election Treaty signed, providing for unification before all-German elections.
31 August	Unification Treaty signed.
12 September	Two Plus Four Treaty signed in Moscow.
13 September	FRG-USSR Treaty on Good Neighborliness, Partnership and Cooperation signed.
1 October	Foreign ministers of the four occupation powers sign agreement on the expiration of Four Power rights in the Federal Republic and Berlin.
3 October	FRG-GDR constitutional and legal union enters force.
5 October	Bundestag ratifies the 2 + 4 Treaty.
11 October	U.S. Senate ratifies 2 + 4 Treaty.
14 October	German-Polish Treaty confirming the existing border along the Oder-Neisse.
2 December	First all-German elections. The CDU/CSU wins with 45.8 percent (SPD 33.5 percent, FDP 11 percent, PDS 9.4 percent). The Republikaner party does not pass the five percent hurdle.

1

The United States, the Soviet Union, Germany and the German Question During the Cold War

This is not a matter of mere apprehensions about some unforeseen and unfavorable development of the situation in Germany itself. The entire structure of the military and political confrontation, everything we associate with the Cold War period, in the postwar years became bound up with Germany, as a geographical concept. So we are not talking about Germany alone, and we are not resolving solely German problems.

—Soviet Foreign Minister Eduard Shevardnadze
at the opening session of the 2 + 4 talks in Bonn, May 7, 1990

THE GERMAN QUESTION, ONCE AGAIN

German questions have never been a matter solely for the Germans. What Germany and Germans have done since the unification of that nation in 1871 have had profound implications for all of Europe and beyond. The division of Germany became the centerpiece of the postwar order in Europe. The end of what Eduard Shevardnadze referred to as an unnatural state of affairs both ended the Cold War era and opened an as yet undefined new epoch.

German unification was the most important single event in the European "year of miracles" (which was actually a year and a half long), beginning with the Polish roundtable in the spring of 1989 and ending with the unification of Germany on October 3, 1990. These events—and the even more momentous ones of 1991, which brought the dissolution of the Soviet Union—marked the close not only of the Cold War but also of the twentieth century itself.

The century was marked by a power struggle for hegemony in Europe and by ideological wars between two forms of totalitarianism (communism and fascism) and democracy and between what was called a "socialist" economic model and that of mixed free economies. It also saw the failure of the attempts of two states (Germany and the Soviet Union) to achieve hegemony in Europe and the entry of America as a European power. The forces and ideologies that will shape the twenty-first century have only begun to emerge from the current one. Their contours are still not clearly discernible.

The story of German unification is, consequently, an important one, as it marks both the end of an historical era and the beginning of a new one. It offers both insights into why the old regime collapsed and portents of what may replace it. German unification had at least two levels: the international and the domestic. This book looks at the former, examining the diplomatic aspects behind the creation of a new state. It does not deal directly with the internal aspects of this story, namely, how the two German states shaped a new political, economic and social order. It concentrates especially on the diplomacy of the states involved in the 2 + 4 negotiations: France, Britain, the German Democratic Republic (GDR), the United States, the Soviet Union and the Federal Republic of Germany (FRG), with closest attention to the last three. It also includes consideration of the roles of Poland and NATO in the broader context.

The 2 + 4 negotiations were a framework within which the Foreign Ministers of the four victor powers of World War II met with their East and West German counterparts. This history is in part a record of that process, but, as the reader will see, goes beyond the negotiations themselves to examine the broader context of the diplomacy that finally resulted in the legal unification of Germany on October 3, 1990.

AMERICAN POLICY AND THE NEW GERMAN PROBLEM

The American public and its leaders have been more relaxed about the prospect of a united Germany than have the people of the countries closer to the Germans. Geography and relative power have provided both distance and security to Americans in their views on and policies toward Germany. With no border disputes to worry about, America could regard a unified Germany as less of a direct threat to its power than the Europeans could.

After the end of World War II, U.S. policymakers quickly rejected the partition or weakening of Germany. They remembered the failure of the Weimar Republic, which followed the 1919 Treaty of Versailles, and wished to avoid any repetition of that unhappy period. The eventual division of Germany was neither the result of World War II nor an objective of American policy. It was the result of a dispute between allies who became adversaries rather than the revenge of a victor over the vanquished—a direct consequence of the breakdown in U.S.-Soviet cooperation. As the Cold War intensified, therefore, the view grew in the U.S. government that in order to establish a new equilibrium in Europe, Western Europe (including West Germany) needed to be stabilized, even at the cost of the division of the Continent and of Germany.[1]

[The division of Germany became a by-product of the broader policy of containment, which in turn was only a new variation of a long-standing American policy aimed at preventing the domination of Eurasia by one power.] Before World War II, the United States had relied upon another great maritime power, Britain, to serve as the balancer of the European system. The inability of Britain to continue to play this role was apparent during the war when two non-European powers, the Soviet Union and the United States, restored the balance disturbed by Germany. The decline of Britain and the replacement of Germany by the Soviet Union as the major threat to European security made the United States a European power and put Germany in a pivotal role again.[2]

The German problem for the United States in the Cold War had thus been transformed from a direct threat to the European balance to an indirect one. Germany was now a threat to the balance if it shifted its weight in favor of the Soviet Union. As Wolfram Hanrieder put it, "Germany replaced Britain as the arbiter of the European equilibrium."[3] The United States had been intent on preventing, therefore, Germany's turn to a policy of neutrality or active cooperation with the Soviets.

Leading American policymakers worried that the division of Germany would play into Soviet hands. Secretary of State Dean Acheson feared a new Molotov-Ribbentrop Pact, and the American High Commissioner in Germany, John McCloy, wrote that although attached to the West, "the Germans cannot help but be aware that the concept of unity comes from the East."[4] It was partly because of this worry that George Kennan, the father of containment and Director of the State Department's Policy Planning Staff, argued in the late 1940s for a neutral but unified Germany. He believed that a continued division would revive German nationalism directed against the occupying powers and would relegate Eastern Europe to the position of an unstable and dangerous satellite.

American policy toward Germany was at the center of its larger European policy. President Harry Truman and his Secretary of State, Acheson, as well as President Dwight Eisenhower and his Secretary of State, John Foster Dulles, came to the conclusion that a strong and unified Western Europe within a divided Continent was preferable to a unified but weak Europe dominated by the Soviet Union. They developed a strategy based upon a policy of strength and a magnet theory of containment. This strategy assumed that a revived and vibrant Western Europe would serve as a magnet toward the East, eventually drawing the USSR's East European satellites toward the West.[5]

Kennan's view of containment was similar to this approach in its assumption that a strong and pluralistic world order would eventually force the Soviet Union to "mellow" and liberalize. However, he saw the Soviet threat as economic and psychological in nature and one that should be met by nonmilitary means. But as the Cold War escalated with the Korean War, American policy began to emphasize military as well as economic instruments in the containment of the Soviet Union and of communism. In Europe this led to the development of an integrated military command within NATO and the rearmament of West Germany. Kennan became a leading critic of this policy on the grounds that it would maintain the division of Germany and therefore of Europe, making Europe a dependency of the United States and resulting in an overcommitment of American resources.[6] Kennan's approach was rejected not only by the American government but also by European leaders who preferred American leadership to a more uncertain alternative. In the words of David Calleo, "Kennan underestimated both the exuberant strength of the United States and, above all, the weakness of the West Europeans."[7]

American policy was not only guided by a desire to counter the Soviet threat to the European balance and thus to keep the Germans from shifting that balance but also by a vision of a postnational Europe. During World War II Dulles had viewed Europe as a "firetrap" due to its divisive nationalism. Americans had been drawn into two European conflicts in the twentieth century because of this nationalism and the inability of the Europeans to control its dangerous effects. U.S. planning and policy in the postwar period was designed to avoid a repetition of these unhappy experiences by promoting European unification through the Marshall Plan, NATO, and later, the European Economic Community.

The German problem was central to this larger postnational project (the term "double containment" has been used to describe this policy).[8] American policy was directed at reviving and rearming West Germany while reassuring the French and other Europeans about German power. Although they worried about other forms of nationalism, particularly the French variant, American policymakers were most concerned about renewed German nationalism.

There remained, as well, a cultural dimension to the German question for postwar Americans. The close link between domestic politics and foreign policy in German history was apparent and needed little elaboration after World War II. Kennan expressed a widespread skepticism about the "German character" when he wrote, "The German people are still politically immature and lacking in any realistic understanding of themselves and their past mistakes."[9] So long as Germany was not a mature liberal democracy it would be distrusted by Americans who, like the Germans, lived in the shadow of the failed Weimar Republic.

The failure of democracy to develop deep roots in Germany was part of a general uncertainty about the German identity. As Renate Fritsch-Bournazel has posed it, "The German question has always been the question of where in Europe the Germans belong: looking westward or wandering between East and West."[10] Unlike the British or the French, the Germans had no history of national identity. Located in the center of Europe and unified late as a nation, the Germans were, as Luigi Barzini described them, mutable—a protean nation.[11] Confronted by cultural currents from both East and West and by a wide variety of political traditions, Germany to many Americans was a land capable of rapid and wild swings. Would postwar Germany be integrated into the West or drift back toward the *Sonderweg,* a special German path between East and West? Would the old ideal of *Mitteleuropa* be revived, an ideal that had great resonance both before World War I and in the interwar period?

Many of these concerns were laid to rest during the formative stages of the Federal Republic by the dominant figures of Chancellor Konrad Adenauer and his Economics Minister, Ludwig Erhard. The American policy of containment paralleled Adenauer's policy of strength. Adenauer gave priority to integration with the West and close links to the United States and relegated national unification to a future in which a strong West was constructed. A Catholic Rheinlander, Adenauer had a Carolinian view of Europe and preferred a little (largely Catholic/Christian Democratic) Europe tied to the United States over a bigger *Mitteleuropa* in which a neutral and Protestant/Prussian-led Germany would live under the shadow of Soviet power. He believed deeply in the desirability of a postnational Europe both as an end in itself and as a means of overcoming the dangers of German nationalism.

Adenauer, however, did secure Western acceptance of the desirability of German unification as a principle of Western policy in return for West

German adherence to the Western alliance. In the so called *Deutschland Vertrag* of 1954, which ended the occupation regime in West Germany, the United States, Britain and France formally committed themselves to German unification, stating in Article 7 that an essential goal of their common policies would be a peace treaty between Germany and its former enemies that would provide for enduring peace. The question of the final borders of Germany would be decided in this treaty.

> Pending the peace settlement, the Signatory States will cooperate to achieve, by peaceful means, their common aim of a reunified Germany enjoying a liberal-democratic constitution, like that of the Federal Republic, and integrated within the European community.[12]

While the harsh choices imposed by the Cold War had pushed the United States to accept integration of part of Germany into the West at the cost of its division, by the early 1960s American policy had begun to accept the notion that the division of Germany was a long-term stabilizing factor. NATO had become the keystone of America's position in Europe, and the integration of the Federal Republic with the West was essential to the viability of the Atlantic Alliance. As Ronald Asmus observed in his study of the German question,

> The FRG's integration into NATO, instead of spurring greater efforts at overcoming the status quo, served as a political palliative, offering a sense of stability and relief that the troublesome German Question had found an acceptable solution, at least for the interim. Western energies were increasingly redirected toward the tasks of political and economic integration and the formation of the European Community.[13]

In addition, the United States was no longer invulnerable to a Soviet nuclear strike on its homeland and thus began to move toward a policy of arms control and détente to lower the risks it carried for Europe. It came to see stability and the status quo as in its interest, and the division of Germany was part of this stabilization policy.

DÉTENTE AND THE GERMAN QUESTION

American and West German policies first came into conflict when the Kennedy Administration reacted passively to the construction of the Berlin Wall in 1961. The strain increased when John F. Kennedy began to pursue a policy of détente with the Soviet Union in the wake of the Cuban missile crisis. Adenauer's always present (if latent) "Potsdam Complex," a fear that the two superpowers would form a new condominium at German expense, was revived. Adenauer moved closer to Charles de Gaulle's France in the twilight of his chancellorship as a hedge against "American unreliability."[14] While this first rift was papered over by the Atlanticist government of Ludwig Erhard, Lyndon Johnson's détente policies strained German-American relations once again.

The Nixon-Kissinger détente, which was a response to the cost of the Vietnam War, the declining American willingness to support an expensive containment of the Soviet Union, the implications of nuclear parity and the less ideological, realist approach of Richard Nixon and Henry Kissinger to global politics, occurred almost simultaneously with Chancellor Willy Brandt's *Ostpolitik* (Eastern Policy). Through the Nixon Doctrine, a policy of "hegemony on the cheap,"[15] the Administration hoped to devolve regional stabilization to regional allies while détente was aimed at stabilizing parity and the arms race at the lowest possible level. Kissinger also believed that détente could transform the Soviet Union from a revisionist to a satisfied power with a stake in the status quo.

This new Soviet-American détente threatened to dissolve the Federal Republic's continuing policy of strength. The West Germans became more and more isolated as such policies as the Hallstein Doctrine (under which West Germany refused to recognize any regime, with the exception of the Soviet Union, which recognized the GDR) looked increasingly anachronistic. Finally, following the accession to power in 1969 of the Social-Liberal coalition under Brandt and the beginning of the new *Ostpolitik* of Brandt and his Foreign Minister and Vice-Chancellor, Walter Scheel, the U.S.-West German gap began to close.

The new *Ostpolitik* was based on the concept of *Wandel durch Annährung* (change through rapprochement). Developed by Brandt's close advisor, Egon Bahr, in the early 1960s, the new approach assumed that the best way to change the West German-East German status quo was to recognize it. Bahr contended that once the West Germans accepted the GDR's existence (even if they did not formally acknowledge it as a separate state) and began to interact with it, the German question could begin to be answered. East Germany and Eastern Europe could gradually be opened to Western influence and be incrementally liberalized.

The *Ostpolitik* was based on the deterritorialization and Europeanization of the German question. It was deterritorialized with the new policy's shift of emphasis from borders to open borders, human contact and human rights. Europeanization required that a new European peace order be created in which pan-European cooperation would replace bipolar confrontation. This meant a diplomacy of accommodation toward the East rather than one of Cold War confrontation, a policy of rapprochement rather than of threats to existing borders.[16]

√ The new *Ostpolitik* contained both stabilizing and destabilizing elements. Bahr had believed that contact between the two Germanies would revive the concept of a common national identity. As he once said, "Nations exists when people meet." In this sense, the new détente policies could be seen as aimed fundamentally at transforming the GDR without destabilizing it in dangerous ways. Following a policy line similar to Kennan's, the Social Democratic Party (SPD) returned to a modification of a strategy suggested in the 1950s by its first postwar leader, Kurt Schumacher, of promoting reunification through détente. It was this dynamic side of *Ostpolitik* that concerned both the East and the West.[17]

On the other hand, the Brandt détente policies had a tendency to freeze or stabilize the national division. As détente became institutionalized during the 1970s and 1980s, the West Germans, at least, grew to accept the fact that the division would not be overcome for a considerable period of time, if at all. For many the German question changed from one of overcoming the division to one of humanizing it and lowering its costs. Making the border permeable replaced the goal of eliminating the border altogether. The division thus became associated with stability and peace, and by the end of the 1970s, the goal of West Germany policy had become one of détente and cooperative security. As Adenauer had warned, the division became an accepted part of the status quo.

When the crisis of détente began at the end of the Vietnam War and peaked after the Soviet invasion of Afghanistan at the end of 1979, U.S. and West German policies diverged again. This time a role reversal occurred as President Ronald Reagan became more hostile to the Soviets than Kennedy had been, while Chancellors Helmut Schmidt and Helmut Kohl became less hostile than Adenauer. Now the United States was confronting the Russians while the Germans were intent on maintaining détente.

The détente imperative became a fundamental principle of West German foreign policy in the 1980s. The West Germans had by then developed a concrete stake in a relaxation of tensions in Europe. Tourist and family visits to East Germany had dramatically increased. Berlin was no longer a center of crisis. The prospects of war on German soil had been perceptibly reduced. Substantially closer West German-East German relations made the division more tolerable and held out the prospect of even closer contact in the future.

American views on détente, in marked contrast, had dramatically changed, beginning in the second half of the Carter Administration. In the wake of new Soviet activism in the horn of Africa and in Angola, the Soviet invasion of Afghanistan and its potential threat to the Persian Gulf (heightened by the crisis in Iran), as well as growing American disillusionment with the strategic arms control process, the Reagan Administration came to office with the belief that détente was a form of appeasement that weakened the American will and the nation's global position. Reagan was intent on reviving American military strength and confronting the Soviets with a rejuvenated America. The Administration went ahead with the deployment of Intermediate Range Nuclear Forces (INF) in Europe, unsuccessfully tried to persuade the Europeans to forgo the construction of a gas pipeline from the Soviet Union, placed sanctions on Poland following the repression of Solidarity in 1981 and announced an ambitious program of space-based defense (the Strategic Defense Initiative or SDI).

West Germany's reaction was to try to insulate détente, and especially the West German-East German relationship, from this growing superpower confrontation. The independent German strategy that had begun under Brandt continued under Schmidt and Kohl, and a significant divergence of German and American policies persisted. Although the Kohl government did deploy the INF missiles, it also continued to pursue *Ostpolitik* with only minor variations.

This new German-American tension eased with the beginning of yet another period of Soviet-American détente, this time initiated by Reagan and Mikhail Gorbachev in the second half of the 1980s. While this new détente disquieted some German conservatives who worried about a new antinuclear Potsdam emerging from the Reykjavik summit and the INF treaty, resulting in the revival of a new variant of German Gaullism, overall it stabilized German-American relations.

The 1980s, however, signaled fundamental changes in the U.S. and German approaches to the German question. For the Germans, including the Christian Democrats (CDU), détente had to precede unification, rather than follow it as it did under Adenauer's policy. The process of détente, including arms control, was now seen as an essential part of conflict management and a safer way of dealing with the national division.[18] For the Americans this divergence on the issue of détente raised old concerns about a neutral Germany or even of a new Rapallo (a new Soviet-German rapprochement). Henry Kissinger, Zbigniew Brzezinski and other influential figures raised the specter of the Finlandization of the Federal Republic and saw evidence for this trend not only in the rise of the antinuclear movement but also in the close nature of West German-East German relations and in tendencies among both the German public and elites toward equivalence or equidistancing (that is, viewing both superpowers as similar or equivalent in their foreign policy behavior and in the threats they posed to peace).

AMERICA AND WEST GERMANY ON THE EVE OF THE GERMAN REVOLUTION

The United States entered the year of German unity with a relaxed attitude toward the German question. While the doubts about nationalism and neutralism that arose during the Euromissile (intermediate-range nuclear forces, or INF) debate had not disappeared entirely, the renewal of détente begun by Reagan and Gorbachev had stabilized West German-American relations. In addition, both nations were ruled by moderate conservative governments, a factor that provided an added element of confidence to the relationship.

The Bush Administration was viewed with far less anxiety by both the German public and leaders alike than had Reagan's. Bush and his team were the type of traditional moderate conservatives the German establishment and much of the public felt comfortable with and were not the less predictable ideologues of the Reagan Administration. Public opinion in the Federal Republic showed a renewed confidence in American leadership and policies, although the tendency of many Germans to view both superpowers as equivalent in their foreign policy behavior remained.

On the American side the concerns about the fragility of German democracy and the Westernness of its political culture that were prominent in the immediate postwar period were no longer present among the majority of the American public and their leaders. West Germany was seen in a series of opinion surveys as both a country where the United States had important interests and one about which Americans had positive emotional feelings.[19] The years of stable democracy in West Germany combined with the image of Berlin as an outpost of the free world and reinforced by the experiences of hundreds of thousands of American military personnel and their families in West Germany had created a positive German image with the American public.

Thus, it was not surprising that as German unification began to emerge at the end of 1989 as a real possibility, international opinion surveys found the American public to be the most supportive of German unity of any people in the West.[20] Democratic demonstrations on the streets of Leipzig, Dresden and other East German cities also appealed to the strong American belief in self-determination.

In spite of the fact that George Bush's Administration had been criticized in early 1989 for lacking "vision" in dealing with the sweeping changes being set in motion by Gorbachev, the U.S. government was not taken entirely by surprise by the fast-breaking events of late 1989 and 1990. Among some of the key leaders in the newly elected Bush Administration there was a sense early on that important changes were underway in the German-American-Soviet trilateral relationship.

Two of Secretary of State James Baker's key aides, Dennis Ross and Robert Zoellick, were preparing for sea changes in foreign policy. Ross, Director of the Policy Planning Staff in Baker's State Department, was already having discussions in the 1970s with his mentor at the Pentagon, Director of Net Assessment Andrew Marshall, over the Soviet threat and about how, as Marshall later recalled, "the Soviet economy was in terrible shape and far worse than most people in the government were aware—and therefore the Soviets were going to be in a progressively weaker and weaker position."[21]

Zoellick, Counselor to Secretary Baker and one of the architects of the diplomacy of German unity, wrote papers for Baker during the transition from the Reagan to the Bush Administrations in which he analyzed the changes in the strategic environment associated with the end of the Cold War. He identified three changes that had special significance for German-American relations: the appeal of Gorbachev in Germany, the importance of generational change and the growing salience of sovereignty concerns in West Germany, by which he meant the German public disquiet over low-flying military airplanes and maneuvers (including those conducted by American and other Allied forces) in German forests and fields. This was what the American Ambassador to West Germany, Vernon Walters, labeled the vestiges of pro-consulship left over from the occupation. As Zoellick later put it, "This was in the back of our minds. How do we manage this critical relationship in changed circumstances?"[22] Some of this thinking was found in the Administration's public pronouncements (issued in a series of Presidential speeches in May), as Bush began to talk about "moving beyond containment" and of a "Europe whole and free."[23]

Behind all of this, as well, was a growing respect for the economic weight of the Federal Republic and for the constructive role it was playing in the European Community. Six months before the opening of the Berlin Wall, at the time of the Brussels NATO summit of May 1989, President Bush was speaking of the United States and Germany as "partners in leadership." Indications were unmistakable that the Germans had replaced the British as the key partner for the United States in Europe.[24]

The NATO summit was a critical event in the evolving new German-American relationship. The main issue on the agenda was the debate over whether NATO should modernize its short-range nuclear forces (SNF) in the Federal Republic. The SNF, which had the tactical mission of countering Soviet conventional superiority, had the disadvantage of having ranges so short that they would land only on German soil. They were seen as essential by many in the Pentagon and in Britain to maintaining the integrity of nuclear deterrence. Their short range, however, created unease among a German public that feared that the SNF would make Germany a nuclear battlefield in an East-West conflict.

Baker had made a tour of NATO capitals early in his tenure as Secretary of State and found that the attitudes on SNF he encountered in Europe were very different than those prevalent in the Washington national security bureaucracies. He recognized that the alliance was headed for a clash on the issue, especially with the Germans, and he began trying to adjust American thinking toward a compromise.

At Brussels, Baker and West German Foreign Minister Hans-Dietrich Genscher were able to achieve an agreement on SNF that put off any decision to modernize these weapons. In April Genscher, who was born in East Germany, had made an impassioned speech to the Bundestag on the topic of SNF:

> ... we are talking about short range systems which can reach the other part of our fatherland. Thus if we are called upon to make such a decision we will not forget this fact and I state this here on my own personal responsibility. The members of the Federal Government have sworn on oath to dedicate their efforts to the well-being of the German people. The obligation deriving from that oath does not stop at the border cutting through Germany. The responsibility for the nation established by the oath does not exclude my native region, the town where I was born, nor the people in the GDR. Indeed it includes them.[25]

The depth of feeling on this issue for Genscher was apparent, and its resolution to his satisfaction helped to create a bond of trust between him and Baker that proved to be vital in the year of German unity.

The SNF prelude set the stage for the larger play that was about to begin. By siding with the Germans the new Administration came into conflict with British Prime Minister Margaret Thatcher, who strongly supported the modernization of SNF. The new American leaders, who had decided that the special relationship the United States had with Britain could remain special but not exclusive, had no desire for the British to play a mediating role between the United States and Europe.

By the spring of 1989 some within the Bush Administration had begun to think about German unification as a realistic policy goal. When Ambassador Walters offered George Ward in April 1989 the job as his deputy, he told Ward that he would find it an interesting assignment because the Berlin Wall would be opened within the year. Walters based his prediction on the belief that Gorbachev, as part of his opening to the West, would take the initiative and open the Wall. The abandonment of the Brezhnev Doctrine, Walters believed, made this inevitable.

A debate had begun within the Administration in the spring and summer of 1989 over what to do about ending the Cold War. One school, centered in the Policy Planning Staff of the State Department, argued that U.S. policy should push for more change in the GDR and for the larger view that the United States should seek to go beyond the Cold War and end the division of Europe and of Germany. Francis Fukuyama, the Deputy Director of the Policy Planning Staff, authored a memorandum over the summer in which he argued that the chain of events beginning in Poland and Hungary would lead to similar changes in East Germany and thus logically result in the end of the division of Germany. He further wrote that the United States should plan on unification or confederation within a year and that it should support this change on the grounds that if it did not promote unification, it would be marginalized by the new Germany and by Europe.

Others, particularly those in the European Bureau of the State Department, believed that the United States should support the policies of the West German government and not get out in front or be more German than the Germans. Brent Scowcroft and his staff at the National Security Council were in favor of promoting unification but urged the United States to be careful and to not get ahead of the German Chancellor.

By early October 1989 a general consensus was reached within the upper levels of the Administration that the United States would support German national aspirations, although there was still disagreement over whether this would be open support for unification or simply for national self-determination. Yet the swiftness of the changes that came from within East Germany startled everyone and opened up a period of creative diplomacy.

OSTPOLITIK, CONTAINMENT
AND THE REVOLUTION OF 1989

Who was vindicated by the unification of Germany: Adenauer or Brandt? Kennan or Dulles? This question, posed by Timothy Garton Ash, is likely to be at the center of a long debate by political scientists and historians:

> There is much to be said for the claim that the East Central European "year of wonders," '89, was a late triumph of Adenauer's "magnet theory"—the idea that the attraction of a free and prosperous Western Europe would sooner or later draw the unfree and impoverished East Germany irresistibly toward it. But could the magnet have exerted its full attractive force if the blocking iron curtain had not first been drawn back by *Ostpolitik* which Willy Brandt launched in the late 1960s? And was it not Bonn's Western but rather its Eastern ties—above all those to Moscow—which directly permitted the transformation of an East German movement for freedom into an all-German state of unity?[26]

The German public and probably most of the German establishment give the major portion of the credit for German unification to Gorbachev. Ronald Reagan and the United States in general are not as frequently cited in this regard.[27] It is certainly true that the unification of Germany was due to a fundamental shift in Soviet policy that accepted a united Germany under largely Western terms. But the more important question remains as to why this shift occurred, and the answers tend to support the view that Western strength combined with a systemic crisis in the Soviet Union were probably the main reasons that Gorbachev changed Soviet strategy.

Ostpolitik and the new *Deutschlandpolitik* of the Federal Republic probably had little to do with the coming of unification in practice if not in theory. If anything they may have stabilized the GDR and the image of two German states in West Germany. They certainly discouraged any possible opposition groups in East Germany both through the West German official legitimization of the Socialist Unity Party (i.e., the East German Communist Party, SED) and through the safety valve provided by emigration to the FRG. West German leaders and public alike learned to accept the division of the nation and to think of an Austrian or two-state solution to the German question. They were as surprised by developments in the GDR as anyone else.

The most effective portion of West German policy was not its détente aspects but rather the model of an alternative society it offered to East Germans, a model presented every night on East German television.[28] This ideal contrasted with an un-ideal reality in the GDR. There was, in addition, the growing dependence of the East German economy on trade, credits and other payments from West Germany.[29] It was this aspect of *Ostpolitik* that made an important difference. When the Revolution of 1989 began on the streets of Leipzig and other East German cities, the GDR leadership was restrained in the severity of its response both by the Soviet Union and by the fear of the consequences for its economic relationship with the FRG. In this regard, as well as in many others, the GDR was not China and could not attempt a Tiananmen solution. Finally, the opening of borders that occurred in Poland and Hungary further undermined the SED. The Hungarians recognized the substantial economic benefits that would accrue if they kept their border to the West open to East Germans. The Hungarians, like the Soviets, knew that their future lay with access to West Europe and especially to West Germany. This was another argument for the magnet theory.

The *Ostpolitik* was important, however, in ending the division of Germany through the legacy of confidence that had been built up between Germans and Russians over two decades of détente. Kohl's National Security Advisor, Horst Teltschik, referred to this in his memoir when he wrote that Kohl "believed it was an especially fortunate coincidence that the relationship between the two nations, as well as the personal relations, had developed so positively."[30]

The events of 1989-1990 also seem both to justify and to undercut Kennan's strategy. On the one hand, Kennan had argued that successful containment would lead to the "mellowing" of the Soviet Union. Whether this would have occurred in Europe without what Kennan believed to be the "militarization" of containment through NATO is uncertain. A policy of neutralizing a unified Germany, which Kennan supported in the 1950s, may have opened up the process of European unification earlier than turned out to be the case, although this is questionable given Soviet policies during that period. It would, however, have resulted in the unification of Germany at a time when German democracy was just beginning, when the European Community had not yet been created and when Germany would have been militarily and psychologically much weaker and living in the shadow of a still essentially Stalinist Soviet Union. This outcome would surely have been less desirable than that which occurred about forty years later, a unified and democratic Germany within a much more cohesive Europe, with a continuing American presence and a weakened Soviet Union.

So while the answer to the original question may be a bit hedged, the Western strategy of strength modified with a few elements of *Ostpolitik* seems to have prevailed. If the United States pursued a policy of "double containment," the West Germans had a policy of dual reconciliation. The Adenauer policy of strength and Western integration, on the one hand, reassured the West and provided Helmut Kohl with a stable core of Western support, especially in the United States. The *Ostpolitik,* on the other hand, reassured the Soviets that the consequences of unification would not be dangerous to their interests. It may have also accomplished the aim set out by one of its architects, Egon Bahr, of keeping the idea of the nation alive through a network of contacts. When the crisis and the opportunity came it was the East Germans who shouted *"Wir sind ein Volk"* (We are one people). Even the West Germans, who were less enthusiastic and more concerned about the costs of unification, responded with support for those leaders who delivered speedy unity. The dense network of contacts that had developed over two decades of *Ostpolitik* kept this sense of common identity, or at least the myth of a common identity, alive. The detailed look at the 2 + 4 process that follows will demonstrate how these elements interacted.

2

A Fortunate Case of Statecraft: Personalities and Processes

THE KEY PERSONALITIES

The international aspects of German unification were essentially the work of eleven men: the chief executives, the foreign ministers and the aides within the foreign ministries of the three countries that shaped the outcome, West Germany, the United States and the Soviet Union. France, Britain, East Germany and Poland played decidedly supporting roles.

On the West German side Chancellor Helmut Kohl and his National Security Advisor, Horst Teltschik, Foreign Minister Hans-Dietrich Genscher and his aides, Frank Elbe and Dieter Kastrup, were the key players. Their counterparts were George Bush, James Baker and Baker's aide Robert Zoellick on the American side and Mikhail Gorbachev, Eduard Shevardnadze and his close aide Sergei Tarasenko on the Soviet side.

This group proved to be a remarkably compatible team, working easily together and with mutual confidence. With the exception of Bush, they were all of the same generation: at the senior level were men in their late fifties and early sixties, and at the working level were men in their forties. Being too young to have fought in World War II, they did not carry the emotional baggage of that war. Their images of Germany were shaped by their experience with the postwar democracy and détente policies of the Federal Republic rather than by memories of the Third Reich.

While they all came of age during the Cold War they were not present at its creation. Having begun their professional political careers after the hot and ideological phase of the Cold War (during the era of détente), they were not deeply ideological but rather "pragmatic." The new Soviet style was

especially noteworthy and important to the smooth flow of the negotiations.⌉
As one senior State Department officer noted early on in the talks:

> One of the things that is very striking about dealing with Shevardnadze and
> Gorbachev right now is that they will listen to your arguments. These are not
> stylized discussions. They tend to be very relaxed. When you make a case that
> they think is reasonable, they will come right back and tell you: "Well you know,
> that's reasonable." And there was quite a bit of that in the discussion on the
> Germanies.[31]

When Kohl met with Gorbachev in Moscow in July 1990, a meeting that
produced the final breakthrough on German unification, he reminded
Gorbachev that they were both of the same generation: "too young during
the Second World War to be personally guilty for it, on the other side, old
enough to have experienced these years. With this background of common
experiences it is our task to take the chance offered by history."[32]

Similarly, Genscher worked easily with both his American and his Soviet
counterparts. He had been transformed from an object of suspicion in
Reagan's Washington where "Genscherism" was a code word for appeasement and neutralism, to a close and trusted partner of James Baker. Although
Genscher was not trusted completely by all Americans, especially by some
in the White House who were worried about his "softness" on NATO and
his close relationship with the Soviets, he and his aides worked smoothly
with the State Department.

Baker's initial reserve toward the Foreign Minister had been removed
during the intense negotiations that produced the Alliance compromise that
he and Genscher had worked out in May 1989 on the future of short-range
nuclear weapons.[33] Baker had decided that it did not make much political
sense to cut out the leader of a key party in the coalition that governed West
Germany. The close, personal working relationship between the two men
was strengthened during the September 1989 UN General Assembly meeting, when Baker tried to persuade the Czechs to find a solution to the crisis
caused by the influx of East Germans at the West German embassy in Prague.

Baker's training and experience as a lawyer and deal maker par excellence
was central to German unification. He was an expert at the managerial side
of politics, having successfully directed a series of national campaigns for
Ronald Reagan and Bush and having served as Reagan's Chief of Staff in
the White House. Often characterized as a "quick study," Baker would form
a clear set of goals and then set out ways to achieve them. He had "an uncanny
sense of how you get people to do what you want them to do."[34] As a Soviet

who dealt closely with Baker during this period later recalled, "Baker was the philosophical mastermind, he was instrumental in explaining with crystal sharpness the philosophy of German unification. He explained the different scenarios and the consequences of each."[35] Baker also gained Shevardnadze's trust by stating what he could and could not deliver, and by delivering on what he promised.

This personal relationship at the top was picked up and nurtured between Genscher, Shevardnadze and Baker's top aides as well. Zoellick, Tarasenko and Elbe all belonged to a younger generation, spoke fluent English and had a non-ideological, problem-solving style. They were approachable men who worked well with each other and who are central to this story.

Hans-Dietrich Genscher, like James Baker, had an ability to find compromises and make deals. Like his country and the small but central party he led, the Free Democratic Party (FDP), the German Foreign Minister was always in the middle—both in domestic politics and in foreign policy. Political survival depended upon prescience and agility. In this sense the Foreign Minister resembled statesmen of smaller nations, such as Jan Masaryk of Czechoslovakia or King Hussein of Jordan.

Genscher also had to rely on his ability to persuade and to gain the confidence of his negotiating partners. He had to win the trust of the Soviets in particular, and did this in part through negotiating directly with Shevardnadze for a total of over 60 hours in 1990.

Genscher's most difficult relationship may have been with his own Chancellor. Unlike Baker or Shevardnadze, Genscher was not a close associate of his chief executive. He was instead the leader of Kohl's Christian Democratic coalition partner, the Free Democrats, or Liberals. His party's support was indispensable to Kohl, who could not muster a governing majority without it, and thus their relationship was only a marriage of convenience.

Partners and rivals at the same time, Kohl used Genscher and his party to fend off the demands of the CDU's powerful ally on the right, Franz Josef Strauss and his Bavarian-based Christian Social Union (CSU), while competing with Genscher for the centrist vote that decides German elections. It was the tactically agile Genscher who led the Free Democratic Party out of its 13-year coalition with the Social Democratic Party (SPD) and into one with Kohl's CDU in 1982, and Kohl was always aware that Genscher was fully capable of reversing his field again.

Until the German Revolution of 1989, Genscher ran foreign policy and left defense policy to Kohl's CDU and the CSU. This frustrated many Christian Democrats who were denied any substantive role in foreign policy and who were left feeling that the small FDP tail was wagging the large CDU dog.[36] This also produced a politically uneven division of labor that was characterized by one of the leading members of the CDU as one in which "Genscher modernizes thinking while we must modernize weapons," referring to the Foreign Minister's role as conciliator while the CDU (with the defense portfolio) had to argue for the draft, new missiles and the never popular defense budget.

However, the Revolution of 1989 suddenly merged foreign and domestic policy and brought Kohl into an arena that previously had been largely Genscher's. Kohl and Genscher were a study in contrasts both in personality and in style. Genscher was a statesman with a worldview that had been developed over the sixteen years he had served as Foreign Minister. He enjoyed the international scene and the peripatetic travel that characterized his career. Kohl, on the other hand, was consumed with domestic politics and was less at ease abroad. Yet they were similar in their tactical skills and political instincts.

Kohl was especially adept at outmaneuvering more attractive and highly regarded rivals within his own party and emerging as the winner. Like Ronald Reagan, his opponents tended to underestimate him, yet he combined an exhaustive knowledge of Christian Democratic party politics with what one observer has described as "a phenomenal instinct for the latent majority."[37]

As a southwestern Catholic and a disciple of Konrad Adenauer, Kohl had less reason to jump on the reunification bandwagon than did the East German-born Genscher. Genscher often referred to his roots in Halle as the wellspring of his interest in the German question and was always more identified with reunification than was Kohl, who, with his Rheinish roots and deep identification with the United States, looked West rather than East.

While Kohl had believed since his youth that German unity was a good thing and would eventually come to pass, he was never a *Deutschlandpolitik* expert, being satisfied largely with delivering Sunday speeches extolling the virtues and inevitability of unification yet following the Social Democrats' general policy of small steps. While he was more open than Willy Brandt or Helmut Schmidt in talking about German unity, raising it openly in his trips to Moscow, he nonetheless received Erich Honecker, General Secretary of the East German communist Party, in 1987 for what was for all intents a state visit.

In addition he seemed to have little political interest in unification. The conventional wisdom prior to 1990 was that the East, with its Prussian, Protestant and Social Democratic traditions, was inhospitable political terrain for the Christian Democrats and that reunification would most likely produce an SPD majority.

Kohl was slow to realize that the opening of the Wall on November 9, 1989 meant rapid reunification. As a politician he was faced with the growing problem of massive emigration, which only accelerated after the Wall's breach, and the consequent need to stabilize the situation. He was pushed as well by the East German Communist leader, Hans Modrow, who spoke early on of confederative arrangements. Kohl only came to see reunification as both inevitable and a winning issue after he began to travel in East Germany in December 1989.[38]

The Soviet leaders all approached the German question with personal scars from World War II. Gorbachev's village had been occupied by the Germans and his father had fought them for five years in the Ukraine. One of his closest advisors, Alexander Yakovlev, walked with a limp from a war wound, and Shevardnadze had lost his brother in the war against the Germans. Yet their reformism took precedence over their personal losses. The already discussed generational factor was also crucial in this regard. Gorbachev represented a new postwar generation of Soviet leaders who remembered the scars of German occupation and war but were too young to let it hinder a new, more cooperative, political relationship.

Gorbachev's personal relations with Honecker and Kohl also played a role in the development of Soviet policy. He began his tenure in power on the worst possible footing with Kohl after the West German compared the Soviet leader to the Nazi propaganda chief Joseph Goebbels because of his skill in propaganda. By 1990, however, this had been forgotten, and the personal ties and trust between the West German and Soviet leaders became quite strong during the negotiation of German unity. Especially important in shaping this warm rapport was a visit that the Soviet leader had made to Bonn in 1989. During that visit, Gorbachev and Kohl spent a long time sitting on a balcony along the Rhein river, talking about their experiences and about the future German-Russian relationship. During the July 1990 meeting in Moscow that led to the Caucasus agreement, Kohl spoke of the 1989 meeting and said that it provided the basis for the relationship of trust he and Gorbachev were to develop.[39]

On the other hand, Gorbachev's relationship with Honecker was just the opposite. Here Gorbachev was dealing with leadership of the Brezhnev generation that was just as encrusted and opposed to new blood and new ideas as its Soviet generational counterpart. Honecker did all that he could to block Gorbachev's reforms from spreading to the GDR, including banning reformist Soviet publications and actively collaborating with the Soviet leader's main rival, Yegor Ligachev. Honecker was so indiscreet as to send Ligachev a letter in which he acknowledged the Soviet conservative's request to publish anti-*perestroika* articles from the Soviet press in East German newspapers. Gorbachev feared what a Soviet specialist on Germany, Vyacheslav Dashichev, described as "a new conservative international" being formed against him with the active collaboration of Honecker.[40]

Shevardnadze saw the unification of Germany as a vital part of the new thinking in foreign policy and of *perestroika* at home. Yet even his role was, in the words of Dashichev, that of someone who drew the consequences (*ein Nachvollzieher*) rather than someone who was out in front (*ein Vordenker*). Soviet policy on German unification consistently was behind events, unlike that of the Americans, which often anticipated them. This was due largely to the intensity of the conservative opposition in the Soviet Union to German unification and the waxing and waning of its influence within the Soviet government. Gorbachev's indecisiveness, which became more apparent in the waning year of his rule, also was important in this regard. According to a close aide of Shevardnadze, Gorbachev was slower than his Foreign Minister to realize the pace events would take, and the history of German unification bears him out.

The domestic context was always preeminent in Soviet policymaking during this period. As a Soviet official intimately involved in the negotiations later related, "The internal background meant more to us than the external one. We knew how to make a deal diplomatically, but we worried about the psychological effect of German unification on the domestic context."[41]

THE PROCESS

The external architecture of German unification was developed in the foreign ministries and executive offices of the three key nations involved. Notably marginal were the defense ministries, the legislatures and the political parties.

At the head of the U.S. government was a President who entered office with more experience in foreign relations than any other president in American history. While often criticized for a "lack of vision," Bush had an intimate knowledge of foreign issues and of the leading international personalities. He was not a strategic thinker but had what the Germans would call *Fingerspitzengefühl*, an intuition for the essence of foreign policy in the tips of his fingers. He placed a great deal of importance on his personal ties to foreign leaders and used one-on-one telephone conversations and personal communications as his primary instruments of diplomacy. He quickly grasped the importance of the developments in Germany and used his close, personal relationship with Kohl to maximum advantage throughout the historic year of German unity.

Bush's top aide on German unification was Secretary of State Baker. Their own close, personal relationship was vital to the success of the diplomacy of German unification. As Don Oberdorfer notes, "It was virtually certain that Baker would never experience the damaging treatment at the hands of the White House staff or rival factions within the administration that Schultz and many of his predecessors had suffered."[42]

Below the President, the State Department, supported by the National Security Council (NSC), was the center of action. Within the State Department, Secretary Baker, his immediate staff and the Policy Planning Staff directed the action while the operational bureaus, especially the European bureau, and the Foreign Service—including the American Embassy in Bonn—were assigned distinctly subordinate roles. This style of operation characterized the general way that Baker had run State. He kept major decisions and strategy within a small group of close advisors and largely excluded the Foreign Service from key decisions.[43]

The Secretary and his top aides believed that the radical pace of change with which they were dealing demanded rapid and more creative approaches than they were likely to receive from the Foreign Service. As one aide put it in an interview, "We inherited a world on the brink of enormous change, and the traditional assumptions were left behind by the new world. Baker wanted to get us out in front of the issues. That's not the kind of thing you're going to get from the bureaucracy."[44] This was especially the case in regard to German unification.

In addition, the closed style of decision making suited both Bush and Baker's patrician or elitist approach to policy and politics. Both were consummate insiders who disdained the need for public persuasion in foreign policy. They both preferred closed negotiations with people they knew to speeches, interviews and other public activities.[45]

Baker's key advisors both on general foreign policy and specifically regarding German unification were Robert Zoellick, the Counselor, Robert Kimmet, Deputy Secretary for Political Affairs, Dennis Ross, Director of The Policy Planning Staff (S/P) and Margaret Tutwiler, Deputy Secretary for Public Affairs. None had an extensive background in European or German affairs but all were close to Baker, having worked for him either at the Treasury or in the White House. The relationship between Zoellick and Ross was especially crucial and was so close that, in Zoellick's words, "one would begin a sentence and the other would complete it."[46] Ross's staff in

Policy Planning also played an important role; Francis Fukuyama and Roger George, a long term governmental specialist on European security, were especially involved. It was this group which came up with the idea of 2 + 4, that is of the two German states dealing with the internal aspects of unification while creating the international settlement of the German question together with the Four Powers (the United States, Britain, France and the Soviet Union).

Two members of the professional Foreign Service, Raymond Seitz, Deputy Secretary of State for European Affairs, and his deputy, James Dobbins, did play important secondary roles in 2 + 4. On the NSC side, the key participants were Brent Scowcroft, the President's National Security Advisor, his deputy, Robert Gates, Robert Blackwill, the chief European specialist at the NSC and two of his aides, Condolezze Rice and Philip Zolikow.

The Bush-Baker foreign policy team reflected the style, experience and values of the President. Its members were non-ideological, pragmatic, moderate conservative "inside the Beltway" players who knew the foreign policy and Washington policy networks and thought in its centrist and incrementalist ways. Like their President, these were people who could be justly accused of "lacking vision" and of being reactive, although many found this to be a virtue following the turbulent Reagan years. Notably absent as well was the sharp infighting between State and NSC that had characterized previous administrations. On German unification a good division of labor developed between State, which managed the 2 + 4 process, and NSC, which tracked the security issues.

Zoellick felt early on that he could manage the complex network of issues involved in German unification and at some point in January established a more regular working group within State. The Department's legal bureau took part in this process and its head, Michael Young, and his staff played an important secondary role in shaping U.S. policy. The lawyers were important for the issues relating to Four Power rights (the rights of the four victor powers over Germany in World War II: Britain, France, the Soviet Union and the United States) and in shaping the final treaty. The legal framework provided by Four Power rights was useful in structuring and channeling the many forces unleashed by the collapse of the GDR. It allowed the United States and West Germany to limit the number of players in the game and thus prevent a proliferation of actors that might have made a quick settlement impossible.[47]

On the West German side, the competition between Kohl and Genscher was reflected in an institutional competition between the Chancellor's Office and the Foreign Ministry reminiscent of the State-NSC relationship in the Nixon, Carter and Reagan years. Traditionally there had been no such competition in Bonn because the Chancellor's National Security Advisor was usually a professional Foreign Service Officer. Chancellor Kohl, however, broke precedent and brought in a close personal aide, Horst Teltschik.

Teltschik was a Christian Democrat who was described by the German press as the German Henry Kissinger, a comparison that pleased him. Fifty years old in 1990, Teltschik was born in the former Sudetenland in Czechoslovakia and grew up in the period after the war in Bavaria. He studied at the Free University of Berlin, where he was active in Christian Democratic student politics while being close to Richard von Löwenthal, a leading Social Democratic intellectual. An officer in the army reserves, Teltschik had served as Kohl's advisor for 18 years. While a close confidant of Kohl, Teltschik had a very poor personal relationship with Genscher and with the Foreign Minister's top aides, and consequently strains developed.[48]

In contrast to the case in the United States, however, Germany's Foreign Office had much greater weight and autonomy due to the German tradition of ministerial competence and the strength of the bureaucracy. While the Chancellor had overall responsibility for the broad direction of policy, the Foreign Minister and his Ministry had operative responsibility.

In addition to Teltschik, Kohl's team included Rudolf Seiters, Teltschik's deputy, Peter Hartmann (a career Foreign Service officer) and Wolfgang Schäuble, the Interior Minister and Kohl's close advisor. Teltschik was the main interlocutor for the Chancellor with Gorbachev during the crucial year of 1990, meeting with the Soviet President six times during the year and laying the groundwork for the July agreement in the Caucasus. He later left the government following unification, after he failed in his bid to be appointed State Secretary in the Foreign Office due to Genscher's unyielding opposition.[49] Within the Foreign Ministry, Genscher's key aides were his political director Dieter Kastrup, and his personal aide, Frank Elbe.

As the dramatic events of 1989-1990 began to unfold, Kohl was a politician in trouble. He had a low standing in the polls and was viewed by many as indecisive and clumsy. He faced a strong and unexpected challenge from the right in the form of the new Republikaner party, which was seizing upon nationalist themes. By moving boldly he could identify his party with the national question as surely as Adenauer and Erhard had linked it to prosperity and recovery four decades earlier, producing a twenty-year-long era of Christian Democratic dominance in the process. Kohl and his aides in the Chancellor's office seized the initiative, beginning with the announcement of the Ten Point Plan for reunification on November 28, 1989, and never lost it.

This new activism by the Chancellor, along with the underlying competitive relationship between the Christian Democrats and the Liberals, resulted in a strained relationship between the two main German actors and their respective bureaucracies. Inter-German relations had been considered a matter of domestic rather than foreign policy in the West German policy process, and the Ministry of Inner-German Relations was headed by a Christian Democrat, Dorothee Wilms. Genscher and the Foreign Office could only become players in the reunification game by bringing in the foreign policy aspects, especially the relationship with the Soviet Union and the Polish border issue. NATO-related issues, however, tended to fall within the purview of the Ministry of Defense, another part of the Christian Democratic portfolio. The Chancellor and the Foreign Minister diverged on some important questions, especially those associated with the Polish border, and Genscher came into conflict with the Defense Ministry over the size of the future Bundeswehr (German armed forces) and their structure in Eastern Germany.

On a number of occasions, Kohl, Genscher and their respective bureaucracies did not communicate with each other, creating problems for their international partners. Baker and Bush had to be sure that *both* German leaders were kept informed of developments, Baker working with Genscher and Bush with Kohl.[50] The White House consistently wanted to keep the Chancellor's office in the forefront of the unification process because of their concerns that Genscher might concede too much to the Soviets, especially in the security area, in order to get a quick deal.

The East German role in the process was both minimized and marginalized by Bonn. The communist Prime Minister, Hans Modrow, coordinated policy with Moscow until the East German elections in March, when he was replaced with the CDU Prime Minister, Lother de Maizière, who became subordinate to Kohl. De Maizière's role was best characterized by a comment he himself made near the end of the unification process, comparing himself to a cuckolded husband, who was always the last one to know.

De Maizière was the leader of a coalition that included the Social Democrats. His Foreign Minister was Markus Meckel, a Protestant minister and leader of the East German SPD. Meckel and his deputy, the Reverend Hans Misselwitz, worked closely with the West German SPD, but were generally pushed along by pressure from the East German people and by the growing power of the West German CDU.

While the West German leaders respected the East Germans for what they had accomplished in the German Revolution, they quickly reached the conclusion that the East Germans were too inexperienced and naive to play a serious role in the diplomatic process of unifying Germany—they were artists and religious leaders with no experience in running a government or in dealing with the complex issues of foreign policy. For example, De Maizière, a professional musician, spent part of his first negotiating meeting on internal unification discussing the German national anthem with the West Germans.[51] Kohl suspected de Maizière of being a left-wing Christian who wished to pursue a social agenda to prove his independence. De Maizière, for his part, resented the takeover of the East CDU by the party in the West, calling the CDU General Secretary Volker Ruehe "arrogant."[52]

In addition, the new East German leaders were prisoners of a bureaucracy that was thoroughly controlled by SED apparatchiks for whom there was no incentive to help a process that would lead to the end of their careers and privileges. The new East German leaders even preferred to be chauffeured in West German official cars, knowing that their own were bugged.[53] Meckel, for example, trusted only three people in a ministry of over one thousand employees.

The West Germans ran the East German show. Meckel found it impossible to get a decision from de Maizière, who would constantly change positions because of pressure or advice from Bonn. Meckel's relationship with Genscher was also strained. While the West German Foreign Minister had a political interest in developing a good relationship with his East German counterpart (because of his desire to develop a favorable profile in the GDR), he did not want the East Germans limiting his room to maneuver. Genscher told Meckel early on, "You should not allow any air to come between us." The two agreed to the forming of a commission to prevent the foreign policies of the two states from diverging.[54] Genscher's aides believed that the new East German leaders were taken with their new power and celebrity. Meckel, in turn, never felt that the West Germans trusted him as a working partner and believed that he was being used solely for media purposes.

The Soviet team was cohesive at the top but divided below the summit. Gorbachev and Shevardnadze worked closely and were the key to the final Soviet decision to acquiesce to German unity. By early 1990 Gorbachev had given up on the Party apparatus and had begun to shift major policy responsibilities to his presidential office and to the ministries. He relied heavily on Shevardnadze and allowed him to negotiate most of the details with his Western counterparts, leaving only the major strategic decisions to himself.

Gorbachev was overwhelmed by the demands of managing the Soviet economy and the nationalities disputes and had little time to worry about the Germans. This accounted in part for the sporadic nature of Soviet policy, jerking back and forth as Gorbachev became more or less engaged. It also helps to explain the reasons for the general assessment by Western participants in 2 + 4 of the Soviet delegation as being the most disorganized and ill-prepared of the six.

Shevardnadze was the architect of German unity, a role for which he was to pay dearly as the target of attacks by conservative opponents in the Soviet Union who blamed him for losing Germany. He managed the process largely through his close aides in the Foreign Ministry, the most important being Sergei Tarasenko, Aleksandr Bonderenkyo, the head of the German Department in the Foreign Ministry and Anatolii Kovalev, the First Deputy Foreign Minister. They faced opposition from a number of hard-liners on Germany, notably from two former Soviet ambassadors to Bonn, Valentin Falin and Yuli Kvitsinsky. The current Soviet Ambassador to Berlin, Vladislav Kacthimosov, was also in this group, although his principal deputy and many of the younger Soviet diplomats in the embassy were reporting that the situation in the GDR was fragile and unsustainable. The center of opposition to German unity was in the International Department of the Central Committee, but this organization was kept out of Soviet policy development during 1990. It was restored to a position of influence only in October 1990, when the conservatives regained a temporary ascendancy in Moscow.

These hard-line elements were urging Gorbachev to use force to save the GDR both in August 1989 and more crucially in October during the Leipzig demonstrations. While it is still not clear what happened, it seems that Shevardnadze insisted that force not be used and that his view prevailed with Gorbachev. It may be years, if ever, before the full story is known, but this decision was probably the most important one Gorbachev made on Germany during this fateful year, sparing not only Germany but also Europe and the United States the possibility of an escalation of conflict.[55]

The military and civilian defense leaders in all the countries concerned were the most skeptical about the need for change in strategic doctrine and force postures and resisted what they viewed as unwise concessions on the defense side at the cost of national security. In the United States, Defense Secretary Richard Cheney was the most outspoken in his doubts about the depth and durability of change in the Soviet Union and argued that the viability of NATO should take priority over any rush for a "peace dividend."

His skepticism was shared by Brent Scowcroft's principal deputy on the National Security Council staff, Robert Gates. (Department of Defense representatives were debriefed by the State Department on the progress of the talks but were not involved in the negotiations.)

The Soviet military and civilian defense leadership was less outspoken but was the group most resistant to giving up the Soviet military position in Eastern Europe. Yet its power, always under close party control throughout the history of the Soviet Union, had probably reached its nadir under Gorbachev. The Defense Minister, Dmitri Yazov, was not a full member of the Politburo, unlike his predecessors in the Brezhnev years, and the military consistently saw its budgets cut and its influence weakened during the Gorbachev years. Marshall Sergei Akhromeyev, who served for a time as Gorbachev's National Security Advisor, was a leading skeptic regarding German policy. (He was to commit suicide in the wake of the failed coup against the Soviet President in August 1991.)

In West Germany, the NATO-oriented Bundeswehr leadership was concerned about any weakening of the American connection and extended deterrence and about a unified Germany being exposed to future pressure from a Soviet Union which would remain, after German unification, the most significant conventional and nuclear power in Europe. The Defense Minister, Gerhard Stoltenberg, although a leading Christian Democrat, did not have a great deal of influence on Kohl. He had been politically damaged by his mishandling of tax reform when he was Finance Minister and by a series of scandals within his power base, the CDU in Schleswig-Holstein. Defense Ministry views were channeled to Kohl, as a result, through key allies in the Bavarian CSU. No Defense Minister, however, would have been very effective in the new milieu. Kohl wanted quick unification, and while he was sensitive to defense concerns, he was not willing to be diverted or delayed from reaching his goal by the Defense Ministry.

The East German *Volksarmee* leaders, politicized and trained in Soviet doctrine, knew that they had no future in a unified Germany dominated by the West. Yet to the surprise of everyone, the new Minister for Defense and Disarmament (as the post came to be called in the de Maizière government), Rainer Eppelmann, a man from the conservative Democratic Awakening coalition partner of the CDU, argued for the maintenance of an independent *Volksarmee* after unification. Whether he was motivated by personal ambition or by a desire to maintain East German autonomy is unclear.

While the Western military had greater cause for contentment than did the Soviet and East German, they, too, had to accept restrictions and cuts beyond those they desired or deemed wise. The West German and American national security teams did work together, however, to reshape the original proposals by Genscher concerning the size of the future Bundeswehr and its deployment in eastern Germany.

The 2 + 4 negotiations should be seen, therefore, as a case of high politics, although not in the classic sense. They were an example of diplomacy run almost exclusively by political leaders and their appointees. Yet they were high politics driven by the mood on the streets in the GDR, a case of political elites reacting to a dynamic situation that was beyond their control but whose energies they channeled through the network of diplomacy. The diplomacy of German unification was typical of diplomacy in the late twentieth century—i.e., conducted by politicians, not diplomats, and done via telephone and private conversations facilitated by jet travel.

As Karl Kaiser described it, 2 + 4 was *"ein Glücksfall von Staatskunst,"* or a fortunate case of statecraft.[56] As he notes, the constellation of leading personalities was extraordinary, both in terms of the participants' talent in dealing with a rapidly changing environment and in terms of their ability to cooperate in the most intensive phase of bilateral and multilateral diplomacy in European history. These were politicians with a rich experience in international politics and a refined acumen for tactics. They were all able to manage, or circumvent, the enormous bureaucracies of their governments and to move these gigantic and often lethargic ships of state with dazzling skill. At least three Queen Marys were turned around in turbulent seas in very short order.

3

At the Dawn of a New Era

THE FOUR PHASES OF DIPLOMACY
OF GERMAN UNIFICATION

The 11 months between the opening of the Berlin Wall on November 9, 1989, and the legal unification of Germany on October 3, 1990, can be divided into four phases.[57] The first phase, which will be called the creation of a new situation, was the period during which the status quo collapsed. This phase ran from the opening of the Hungarian border with Austria to East Germans in September until the middle of January. The pivotal events of this phase were the opening of the Berlin Wall on November 9, the announcement of Kohl's Ten Point Plan for German unity on November 28 and the collapse of the Modrow government's authority in mid-January. During this period it became clear to the major players that a new situation was emerging that called for a creative policy response but that the nature of that response was still to be decided.

2) In the second, or blueprint, phase, a design for the process by which a new situation would be created was developed. This phase began in mid-January 1990 and ran through the Camp David meeting between George Bush and Helmut Kohl in late February. It was during this period that the 2 + 4 mechanism was developed and accepted by all the key powers. The main events in this phase were the meetings between Baker and Genscher in early February, the Kohl-Genscher-Gorbachev meeting in Moscow on February 10, the Ottawa Open Skies meeting in mid-February and the Bush-Kohl meeting at Camp David.

3) A third, active negotiating phase followed during which a settlement on German unification was reached. This period ran from the late February, following the Camp David German-American summit, to the conclusion of the Soviet-German agreement in the Caucasus in mid-July, the defining

event. This phase was characterized by the 2 + 4 negotiations in addition to an ongoing trialogue among the West Germans, Soviets and Americans.

4) A final wrap-up or ceremonial stage ran from the conclusion of the Caucasus Agreement through the 2 + 4 meetings in Paris and Moscow and the final treaty signing in Moscow on September 12 to the signing of the Trans-Atlantic Charter in Paris in November.

THE CREATION OF A NEW SITUATION
(SEPTEMBER 1989 - JANUARY 1990)

The first phase of German unification ran from the opening of the Hungarian border with Austria to East Germans on September 11 through mid-January. It was during this stage that a consensus emerged among the key players that German unification was a historical inevitability but that it would probably take five years or more to accomplish. The major actors agreed that they needed to shape this inevitability in a way that would be most compatible with the interests of all and with the requirements for a post-Cold War European security arrangement.

While many analysts and officials in the key governments involved were beginning to think about the momentous changes in Europe and their implications for the German question, all the governments were taken by surprise by the German Revolution of 1989. Most had anticipated changes in Soviet policy, but few foresaw an internal upheaval in the GDR.

Soviet Cold War policy on the German question had one consistent goal: "to prevent the resurgence of a strong united Germany not under Soviet influence."[58] Under Stalin this policy kept open the option of dangling the possibility of unification in front of the Germans in exchange for neutrality. This policy option had the advantage, from the Soviet viewpoint, of preventing the unification of Western Europe under American leadership.

The East German uprising of June 1953 and the Soviet suppression of it, however, increased the Soviet stake in a separate GDR and lead the Soviet Union to adopt a two-state policy instead.[59] Over the Cold War period East Germany became Moscow's most valuable and reliable ally, a bulwark of both the Warsaw Pact and the Council for Mutual Economic Assistance (COMECON). The GDR was the source of high technology for the USSR and became the keystone of the Soviet position in Central Europe.

As détente developed with both the United States and the FRG in the 1970s, the Soviets began to cultivate an interest in better relations with the West Germans. *Ostpolitik* helped to stabilize and legitimize the status quo in Europe, including the recognition of the GDR as a sovereign state. Better

Soviet relations with the FRG also opened the window to the West a little wider, giving the Soviets and their satellites more access to Western markets, aid, credits and technology. West German loans to Eastern Europe, especially to Poland and the GDR, subsidized these failing economies and relieved the Soviets of some of the burden of empire.

When the crisis of détente deepened in the 1980s, the Soviets began to see possibilities of loosening West German ties to the United States and of encouraging a more differentiated and independent West German policy.[60] Yet Soviet flexibility remained limited by its relationship to the GDR. The closer Moscow moved to Bonn, the more nervous East Berlin became. The East German leadership was schizophrenic regarding this triangular relationship, having developed a concrete stake in good relations with the FRG at the same time, and thus continued to pursue German-German détente even when Soviet policy tried to isolate West Germany in the mid-1980s.

Mikhail Gorbachev's accession to power came at this delicate point. The Soviet leader seems to have shaped his grand strategy around the premise that Western power was accelerating at an exponential rate while the Soviet Union was stagnating. If these trends went unchecked, the Soviet Union would cease to be a superpower by the early part of the next century, left behind in the increasingly decisive race of technology by the United States, Japan and a newly dynamic Western Europe.

Domestically, the Brezhnev-era policies had not only done nothing to reverse the decline of the Soviet economy but had also accelerated the pervasive corruption of that society. Internationally, Brezhnev's attempts to take advantage of America's weakness in the immediate post-Vietnam War period had reawakened American resolve and produced an administration that threatened to convert American technological superiority into military advantage. While such key American allies as Japan and the nations of Western Europe were prospering, the Soviet satellites were becoming an ever more debilitating drain on Soviet resources. In addition, the Soviet occupation of Eastern Europe only tended to solidify the American position in Western Europe and block Eastern access to Western technology, credits and markets.

Gorbachev's concept of a "Common European Home" was part of his strategy to change this disadvantageous correlation of forces. Gorbachev's vision was of a Europe in which the Soviet Union could be in the cultural, political and economic mainstream rather than in the ghetto. Like Peter the Great and other Russian modernizers before him, Gorbachev saw the West as the model for Russia, especially as the First World was entering a new technological revolution. Soon there would be no Second World—only the First and the Third Worlds would remain.

Gorbachev was able to come to this conclusion and to win at least the acquiescence of the Party, the military and the KGB to his approach because of the clear failure of Brezhnev's policy of intimidation, especially in West Germany. Gorbachev was, and here *Ostpolitik* made a difference, also able to point to a new Germany and to minimize the threat it could pose to the Soviet Union.

It is probable that Gorbachev and Shevardnadze did not plan on a reunified Germany as the price of this strategy. In the early years of Gorbachev's rule (between 1985 and 1988), in the words of a leading German analyst of Soviet policy, he "continued the previous policy of attempting to isolate and circumvent West Germany, presumably to 'punish' it for its role in legitimizing the stationing of U.S. medium-range missiles in Western Europe and supporting the idea of strategic defense."[61] He deeply resented Kohl's characterizing him as a modern-day Goebbels and studiously avoided visiting Bonn until 1989.

Gorbachev's policy toward Bonn began to change as his domestic policies became more radical. He apparently came to the conclusion in 1988 that his attempts to reform the Soviet system were not working and that deeper and more fundamental changes were necessary. New thinking on the international level was thus accompanied by a more radical version of *perestroika* at home. Concurrent with the new international approach was a rethinking of Soviet military strategy and security policy that aimed both at reducing the threat posed to the Soviet Union by nuclear weapons and SDI and at reducing the ruinous drain of the military-industrial complex on the Soviet economy.[62]

For all these reasons, the new Soviet leaders came to the conclusion that the inclusion of the Federal Republic was central to their new approach to the West. This reposed the classic question of Soviet postwar policy on Germany. As Hannes Adomeit observed, "Inclusion of the Federal Republic in wider East-West cooperation, however, was likely to lead to greater West German penetration of the East and a reduction of Soviet influence and control in Eastern Europe."[63]

Gorbachev seems to have begun his new policy on the German question with the goal of creating a more stable and less costly East Germany led by Gorbachev-style leadership under the direction of a "reformist" such as Hans Modrow, a leading reformer within the East German SED. Gorbachev had come to see Erich Honecker's regime as a carbon copy of Brezhnev's and was angry at Honecker's attempts to resist his reforms both in East Germany and in the Soviet Union itself through Honecker's alliances with Gorbachev's conservative opponents.

Although a debate was going on within the Soviet foreign policy establishment about the viability of East Germany and the desirability of a divided Germany for Soviet interests, the majority view within the Soviet government on the eve of the German Revolution, according to Vladislav Dashichev, an important dissenter from the official policy, was that the GDR was stable and that German division served Soviet interests.[64] A more open but still separate East Germany, be it under communist or noncommunist rule, maximized Soviet interests by lowering the costs of supporting the GDR and removing barriers to better relations with the FRG without opening up the security dilemmas posed by a unified Germany.

The conventional wisdom, held most firmly in West Germany and diffused to its allies, was that the GDR was not Poland. It had no strong opposition movement, and its dissenters had been exported to the West. The secret police, the Stasi, intimidated and controlled the society more thoroughly than any other in Europe with the possible exception of the Securitate in Romania. The East German political culture was a passive one, rooted in centuries of authoritarianism, beginning with Prussia's monarchy led by the Junkers, soldiers and bureaucrats, followed by totalitarianism of the National Socialists and later the Communists. The East Germans had created a "niche society," where everyone found his or her place, kept quiet, went along and received, in return, the benefits of the strongest communist economy in the world and its extensive social welfare network.

A few cracks in this facade began to appear in the spring and early summer of 1989. The local elections of May 1989 were widely seen by many East Germans as a rigged travesty. While this view had been prevalent for all previous East German elections, this election was different because free elections were occurring in Poland and were in sight in Hungary. A campaign to withhold or spoil ballots in the May election was well known and supported by enough people to make the reported 99.9 percent turnout an obvious fraud.

In July Honecker's heir apparent, Egon Krenz, visited Beijing and praised the Chinese leaders for their action in Tiananmen Square. This provoked further outrage among a less and less passive populace. Summer vacation trips were only possible to Czechoslovakia and Hungary, and many thousands of East Germans decided individually to prolong their stay in Hungary to try to cross the newly opened border with Austria. The Hungarian government made the momentous decision on September 11 to allow the East

Germans to leave Hungary for Austria, a decision which began the German Revolution of 1989.

According to the testimony of Kohl's National Security Advisor, Horst Teltschik (who served as the Chancellor's point man on Hungary), Kohl agreed with Hungarian Foreign Minister Gyula Horn and Premier Miklos Nemeth during 1989 visit to Bonn on the date the Hungarian border would be opened to the West. Kohl assured the Hungarians that the Federal Republic would compensate them for any losses they might incur in retaliation for their action from the GDR government.[65] The Soviet leadership, at least according to a close aide to Shevardnadze, while not specifically asked for permission by the Hungarians, approved of the decision to open the frontier ex post facto.[66]

This action opened up a floodgate of refugees, as the West Germans knew it would, which led to a crisis as the East German government began to require visas for visits to Hungary. The West German embassy in Prague became the new magnet for East German refugees. By September 30, over 3,500 East Germans had crowded into the embassy. Genscher was able to convince East German leaders to allow these people to go to West Germany via train, although only on the condition that they pass through East Germany. This gesture of East German sovereignty backfired when large crowds stormed the railroad station in Dresden attempting to board the trains.

It was at this point that another train, that of German unity, really left the station, and the situation in East Germany became untenable. The demonstrations in Leipzig, which had begun on October 2nd, spread to other cities, Krenz replaced Honecker as leader of the SED and Modrow became Prime Minister. The GDR was dissolving.

The final act of a sovereign East Germany was to open the Berlin Wall on November 9, 1989. Even now it remains unclear what the East German government had really decided to do. According to Soviet sources, Shevardnadze had pressed the East German Foreign Minister for weeks without any apparent effect to open the Wall, at least as a short-term safety valve action. Then suddenly, the Soviets received notice of the decision from the East German leadership just before it was announced to the public.[67] On November 9, the SED Politburo met and decided to further ease travel restrictions to West Germany by issuing new travel permits. When the SED's press spokesman, Günter Schabowski, made this announcement, he was rather ambiguous and seemed to say that the Wall would be opened immediately. People began to show up at the exit points, and perplexed border guards frantically phoned for orders. Left without any direction, some guards took the initiative to let the growing crowds through. In this sense, the East German people, rather than the government, opened the Wall.

The attempts of first the Krenz and then the Modrow governments to stabilize the GDR by opening it up were clearly failing. The chant in the streets changed from "*Wir sind das Volk*" ("We are the people") to "*Wir sind ein Volk*" ("We are one people"). The East German public put pressure on the communist government through a combination of weekly demonstrations and mounting emigration.[68]

The West Germans were caught completely by surprise. They had had no prior consultations with GDR officials and no intelligence warnings. The Chancellor had just begun an important visit to Poland, a trip he had to interrupt for a day to fly to Berlin. Genscher realized within a week of the opening of the Wall that unification would come soon and believed by December 1989 that it would be accomplished within a year. As one of his close aides described it, it was a political rather than a diplomatic logic which led the Foreign Minister to this assessment earlier than any of the other key participants. During his trip to Prague at the end of September, Genscher palpably felt the strength of the desire of the East Germans in the West German embassy compound to risk everything for escape. On the train that took four thousand East Germans from Prague through the GDR to West Germany he saw banners of support in the windows of many apartments as well as the approving looks cast even by East German officials toward their fleeing compatriots.[69]

On November 17, a week after the Wall opened, Genscher was standing in a church in his hometown of Halle being introduced by a local pastor who had been active in the opposition to the SED regime. During the introduction, the pastor lamented the loss of idealism and observed that the star of Mercedes was replacing the cross of Christ. The assembled crowd was audibly and visibly uneasy and unhappy with this view, and this mood was picked up immediately by the sensitive political antennae of the Foreign Minister.

Although there was hope and anticipation, the West German leadership was also deeply concerned. From the West German perspective, the most dangerous phase in the GDR ran from October 8, when the demonstrations began in Leipzig, to the opening of the Wall on November 9. It was during this period that the West Germans were most fearful that either the Soviets or the East Germans would use force to try to stabilize the GDR and prevent either a revolution or attacks upon Soviet military personnel and installations.

The Chancellor's office had been approached by an SED emissary, Alexander Schalk-Golodkowski, in October with an offer to dramatically increase travel possibilities for East Germans in return for substantial West German financial support. Kohl responded to this offer in his November 8 report to the Bundestag on the state of the nation, when he clearly proclaimed that he was ready to support real reforms with substantial financial help. But he also made it clear that "cosmetic corrections" would not be sufficient and that he would not stabilize the old system.

Hans Modrow was named Prime Minister on November 13 and immediately tried to relieve the public pressure by talking not only of internal reform and free elections but also of a closer relationship with the Federal Republic, implying a confederation by speaking of a "Community of Treaties" with West Germany on November 17.

These developments within the GDR were accompanied by signals from the Soviets that they were open to radical changes in the German-German relationship. The visit by a leading Soviet official, Nikolai Portugalov, to Horst Teltschik on November 21, was crucial, according to Teltschik, who called Portugalov a "seismograph of the political climate in Moscow." During the visit, Portugalov made it clear that the Soviet leadership not only identified with the developments in the GDR and saw them as compatible with *perestroika,* but was willing to entertain a wide variety of future alternatives for German-German relations, including confederation. He asked Teltschik for a reaction to these possibilities from the Chancellor. Teltschik passed this information on to Kohl, observing, "If Gorbachev and his advisors were discussing the possibility of reunification and had discussed questions related to it, then it was high time that we no longer keep this locked up in a closet, but rather go on the offensive."[70]

THE TEN POINT PLAN

The West German response was Chancellor Kohl's Ten Point Plan, announced to the Bundestag on November 28. The Kohl plan was a relatively modest proposal for the establishment of a number of joint economic, environmental and other commissions, but it held out the prospect of a federation after a period of confederation. This, however, would only be possible once a democratically legitimate government existed in the GDR. Kohl had hoped to give East Germans enough hope in the meantime to provide them with an incentive to stay in the GDR without raising fears throughout Europe that the Germans were pushing for reunification at the cost of broader stability. Although cautiously, the Plan set out an outline for a reunified Germany and encouraged Germans in both Germanies to take reunification seriously.

The Kohl Plan was developed within the Chancellor's "kitchen cabinet," primarily by the Chancellor, Teltschik, Kohl's deputies Peter Hartmann and Claus Duisberg (chief of the negotiating team for German unity) and three speech writers: Norbert Brill, Michael Mertes and Martin Hanz.[71] Genscher and the Foreign Ministry were not consulted and were given notice of the Plan's contents only on the afternoon before Kohl's speech was delivered. The Western allies likewise were not consulted and were informed only after the speech was given to the Bundestag.[72]

The Ten Point Plan was a reaction not only to developments in the GDR but also to those within the FRG and in Europe. Kohl was concerned that if he did not get out in front on the national issue, the Four Powers, especially France and the Soviet Union, might attempt to stabilize East Germany in pursuit of a two-nation solution. French President François Mitterrand had announced his intention a few days prior to the Kohl speech to visit East Berlin in December, and the upcoming Malta superpower summit held out the prospect of a U.S.-Soviet condominium, which might slow the drive to reunification.

To add to these concerns, Kohl was already being criticized at home for lacking a German policy concept. In mid-November two leading Social Democrats, Egon Bahr and Günter Gaus, had called for a Four Power conference to clarify how much freedom the two German states had in dealing with each other.[73] In the words of one of Kohl's aides, "There was a demand, where is the master plan?" The Chancellor was worried that either Genscher or Willy Brandt might seize the national issue for his party.[74] President Richard von Weizsäcker, a Christian Democrat, was concerned that if no party picked up the issue, the radical right-wing Republikaner party would, and the weekly newsmagazine *Der Spiegel* warned that the Republikaner were planning to make reunification a central issue in the upcoming Bundestag election campaign. The Republikaner theme was that Germany should live within the borders of 1937. In the words of its leader, Franz Schönhuber, "Germany should be a neutral country, but with its own nuclear weapons."[75] Kohl and his party had been slipping in the public opinion polls until the changes began to occur within the GDR over the summer. The Chancellor saw that reunification could be the issue to pull his political fortunes out of the doldrums.[76]

During the period leading up to the development of the Ten Point Plan, a number of Kohl's advisors had urged him to go immediately to East Germany while others argued that he find a structure for the new situation.

In the week preceding the formulation of the plan, Kohl and Teltschik spoke about how to create such a structure for shaping unity. They decided to reject a confederation because this would be based on the recognition of two states and because it had been an idea not only of Modrow but also much earlier, of the first East German leader, Walter Ulbricht. They both concluded that a confederation might be seen as an endpoint rather than as a transition and decided on the phrase "confederative structures" instead. This phrase, along with Modrow's *Vertragsgemeinshaft* (community of treaties), conveyed the sense of movement toward federation. At this point Kohl still thought that unification was at least three to four years away.[77]

The plan was essentially developed over a week with the Chancellor making substantial revisions to a draft developed by his staff over the weekend prior to its delivery. It was opposed initially by the German policy experts, Seiters and Duisberg, who were worried about its effects on developments in the GDR and internationally. They argued that the time was not right and that such a plan could be counterproductive.[78] These objections were overcome as the draft progressed. The plan was announced to the public in a statement to the Bundestag as part of the budget debate on November 28. The Chancellor's staff decided not to involve the Foreign Office for fear that Genscher would take credit for the idea. The point was to show Kohl's leadership.

The West German reaction to Kohl's Plan was generally positive. Despite the lack of consultation, Genscher welcomed the Plan and stated that it represented a national consensus. The SPD response from the floor of the Bundestag, delivered by Karsten Voigt, the party's foreign affairs spokesman, was also positive, although Voigt contended that at least two other points needed to be added: a renunciation of short-range nuclear weapons on German soil and a clear and unequivocal declaration on the inviolability of Poland's western borders.

In East Germany, both Krenz and Modrow welcomed the ideas of the commissions and of confederation as long as the sovereignty of the GDR remained intact. The leftist opposition, especially the new Eastern SPD leaders and members of New Forum, the group that helped to spawn the East German revolution, defended the need to maintain a separate East German identity. A coalition of 30 prominent opposition leaders appealed to East Germans to maintain their country's independence and avoid a "sellout of our material and moral values."[79]

The Initial American Response

Outside the Federal Republic the first reaction of the key powers was resentment over not being consulted in advance of the speech and a view that Kohl was moving too fast. Kohl's staff had briefly discussed whether to inform the allies prior to announcement of the plan but decided this was not necessary. Their reasoning was that Article 7 of the so-called *Deutschlandvertrag,* or the Paris Protocol on Termination of the Occupation Regime in Germany, and the general policy of NATO committed the West to the peaceful and democratic reunification of Germany. Thus, the allies did not need to be consulted on something to which they had already agreed. These aides were surprised by the allied reaction to the Ten Point Plan.

The American reaction was guardedly supportive, with State Department spokeswoman Margaret Tutwiler stating that "it would be going too far" to say that the United States endorsed the plan because it had not yet had an opportunity to study it. She went on to add, however, that Kohl was "responding to the deepest aspirations of his people for German unity" and that the United States had long shared this goal.[80]

The American government, in any case, had been urging the West Germans to move to the forefront on the German question. During a visit to Washington the week before the Ten Point Plan was announced, Bush told Genscher that Bonn must take the lead on the national issue, saying that the German question was a "matter for the Germans." The Administration was not prepared to follow the preferences of some its European partners and use its superpower status to interfere with the politics of German unity.[81] The only condition that the American President placed on his support was that German unification occur peacefully. Genscher assured Bush that German unity would not be resurrected as "a roaring lion but rather as a dove of peace." He added, however, *"Wir sind ein Volk."*[82]

Kohl eased any concerns the Americans may have had by sending a long message to Washington explaining the plan and following this up with a lengthy phone conversation with President Bush. The United States during this period was increasingly anxious that the rapid pace of change in East Germany could destabilize the country and undercut the move toward democracy. The West Germans had been urging U.S. policymakers not to hype reunification because this would make the Soviets nervous. Larger fears of a confrontation were also on the minds of American policymakers. As one National Security Council staffer remembers, the NSC during this period was worried about rear guard actions by the Stasi or about attacks on Soviet soldiers leading to a counterreaction. The U.S. government did not want to rub the Soviets' noses in their defeat and possibly undermine Gorbachev and his policies.[83]

American policymakers, however, did not seriously consider attempting to stabilize the GDR to the point where a two-state solution would be the outcome. Bush and Baker were sensitive to the mounting criticism in the United States that they were not responding adequately to the dramatic changes in the Soviet Union and Eastern Europe. They had, in addition, recognized by the May 1989 NATO summit that Germany was now the key power in Europe and that the process of European integration had to be supported as a means of channeling this power in a constructive and non-nationalist direction. Bush had spoken then of the German-American relationship as one of "partners in leadership." This theme was reinvoked as a "new Atlanticism" at the NATO summit in early December, following the Malta summit. As one American observer wrote at the time, "Bush's meaning was clear to those attending the NATO summit: Britain and Margaret Thatcher will play a less significant role in Bush's new alliance architecture. West Germany and the European Community will now be central to America's political and security calculations in Europe."[84]

The developments in East Germany provided an urgent impetus for this policy and pushed Bush and Baker toward a more rapid acceptance of change in the postwar structure of Europe than they had anticipated. To the Bush Administration the question of German unification was, as it had been in the immediate postwar period, less important than the creation of a new European order. At the NATO summit Bush said, "German unification should occur in the context of Germany's continued commitment to NATO and to an increasingly integrated European Community."

America's new policy was further spelled out by the President in his meeting with the Chancellor after the Malta summit by four principles regarding German unification. These were: a) that the principle of self-determination be respected; b) that it occur as part of a broader process of European integration which included NATO and the EC; c) that it be gradual and peaceful and regard the interests of other Europeans; and d) that it should occur with respect for the inviolability of borders as stated in the Helsinki Final Act.[85] During this meeting President Bush informed the Chancellor of the American commitment to fully support German unification. From this point on the West Germans were confident of the backing of the United States.

The four principles were further articulated by Baker in his speech of December 12, 1989, delivered in West Berlin. In the speech Baker argued that the end of the division of Europe meant that a new architecture was needed for a new era and that this new structure must accomplish two main purposes. First, there must be "an opportunity to overcome through peace and freedom the division of Berlin and of Germany." Second, "the architecture should reflect that America's security—politically, militarily and economically—remains linked to Europe's security."[86]

This "New Atlanticism" required new missions for NATO, including a shift in the alliance toward arms control and other cooperative structures in Europe and closer alliance cooperation on regional conflicts. Both the Conference on Security and Cooperation in Europe (CSCE) and the European Economic Community could play valuable roles in this new architecture. Baker strongly supported the process of European economic and political integration in his speech and proposed a closer U.S.-EC relationship in the future.[87] The purpose of the Berlin speech, according to one of its architects, was to create a "safe harbor" (drawing on a term from tax law) that protected against certain dangers. The four principles of the Brussels summit were restated by Baker in an attempt to encompass Kohl's ten points while taking European concerns into account.

Although the Administration's position by December was already one of full support for German unification, there were still some missteps and internal disagreements. The Soviets, concerned about the pace of events in the GDR, called for a Four Power meeting of the Allied Control Council in Berlin. The American government was divided over how to respond to this proposal. On the one hand, the Americans did not want to be seen as attempting to revive Yalta. On the other hand, the Soviets were telling the Americans that they were concerned that the security situation could get out of control and that violent incidents might not then be avoided. They stated that they "would be obliged to use force" if this occurred. Shevardnadze later confirmed that some in the military and the KGB were urging that force be employed to prevent the fall of the East German regime. Four Power rights could become a sticky issue in such a crisis. The U.S. government agreed to the meeting on the basis of what an American official involved in the decision said was a "desire to cushion things with the Soviets." The West Germans were consulted and had agreed as well to the meeting, which took place on December 10. All went well except for the photograph taken at the end showing the four ambassadors together in front of the building that housed the Allied Control Council, an image which created such a bad impression in West Germany that Vernon Walters described it "the worst photograph of the year." The images of the Four Powers representatives standing together in front of a building which represented occupation authority reinforced German fears of a new deal to block German unity. Aides to both Genscher and the Chancellor referred later to this episode as reviving German concern over a new Yalta.

After his Berlin speech, Baker paid a short—hastily arranged—visit to Potsdam and met with Modrow as well as with leaders of the Protestant opposition, after a meeting with the American Ambassadors to the two Germanies, Vernon Walters and Richard Barkely, and the U.S. Minister in Berlin, Harry Gilmour. Barkely was successful in convincing Baker to meet with Modrow, arguing that the situation was brittle and that the Modrow government was the last line of authority. Baker decided to go once he realized that the Soviets had not put their troops on alert and knowing that both Kohl and Mitterrand had planned meetings with Modrow. During his meeting with Modrow in Potsdam, Baker made it clear that the United States would hold Modrow to a timetable for free elections, and Modrow committed himself to this process.

Although the visit was not intended to leave open a two-state solution, some in the State Department, including Vernon Walters, opposed the visit, fearing it would leave the impression among some in West Germany that this was its intent. The disagreement over the Baker visit to East Germany underscored a difference in analysis between the United States embassies in Bonn and Berlin. The embassy in Bonn was, unsurprisingly, more sensitive to West German concerns and perceptions and did not want to do much to stabilize the GDR. The embassy in Berlin was fearful of the impact of rapid change both on stability and on the ability of the East Germans to manage their own revolution. As it turned out, the West Germans, reassured by Bush's pledge of support, were not concerned about the Americans in this regard and viewed the Baker trip as helpful.

By Christmas 1989, American policy had made the fundamental choice to swim with the tide toward unification and to build a stable Europe around a unified Germany. The only preconditions for the United States were that a unified Germany remain a member of NATO and that the security interests of its neighbors (i.e., the Polish border) be met. The NATO precondition seemed to many both inside and outside the government at the time as unrealistic. The working assumption seemed to be that the Soviets would never accept this and that the Germans would compromise on NATO in return for unity. Many in Germany believed the NATO precondition to be a deliberate obstacle to unification.[88]

The American decision to back the West German government in seeking unification and even, according to some in the American government, to accelerate the process "delegitimized" the opposition to Kohl's policies both within the Federal Republic and in the West. Genscher found it difficult to

present himself as more responsible than Kohl, whom he pictured as danger-
ously speeding up the unification train. Foreign opponents of unification,
notably British Prime Minister Margaret Thatcher, who in early December
was making statements discouraging quick German unity, were neutralized
as well by the American policy.

The Soviet Response

The reactions in other key capitals were different from that of Washington
and were generally directed at finding ways of maintaining a divided
Germany under new conditions. The Soviet leadership became increasingly
nervous as events began to accelerate in the GDR after the opening of the
Wall. Shevardnadze's initial response to the Ten Point Plan was to complain
about what he characterized as an artificial acceleration of developments that,
in turn, was causing confusion and could lead to unforeseen consequences.
He called the GDR "a reliable ally and important guarantor of peace and
stability in Europe."[89] After a discussion with Genscher of each of the ten
points, the Soviet Foreign Minister referred to the idea of a fundamental
transformation of the social and economic system of the GDR as a "direct
Diktat" from Bonn, while Kohl's idea of a confederation "could only lead
to confusion."[90] These views were echoed by Gorbachev and other leading
Soviets. Foreign Ministry spokesman Gennadi Gerasimov reacted to the Ten
Point Plan by stating, "There is not one country in Europe today that would
thirst for German reunification because of the questions it raises for stability.
It is not on the agenda."[91] During a speech in Rome just prior to the Malta
summit Gorbachev warned that the West would be making a fatal mistake if
it sought to exploit political upheavals in Eastern Europe to proclaim the
collapse of socialism. He also stated in a Milan press conference that German
reunification could only be considered within the Helsinki process, and while
he did not rule out reunification, he stated it was "not of urgent international
importance."[92]

Gorbachev told visiting West German officials that East and West Germans could live as closely together as they wished but that the question of
state unity was prohibited.[93] He reiterated his warnings about "any artificial
acceleration of the process" of German unification at the Malta summit. As
he spoke, however, the Krenz Government was resigning in East Berlin
following revelations of massive corruption in the Honecker regime and
public protests. Key SED figures were arrested, the leading role of the party
was revoked from the East German constitution and Stasi offices were being
occupied by citizens. A power vacuum had been created in the GDR that was

never really to be filled again. East Germany had begun its free fall toward unification.

The Soviets continued to attempt to gain control over events rather than leave them to the Germans. They called for a Four Power meeting in Berlin, the first in 18 years. Gorbachev told his Central Committee on December 9 that "we will see to it that no harm comes" to East Germany. "It is our strategic ally and a member of the Warsaw Pact. It is necessary to proceed from the postwar realities, including the existence of two sovereign German states. Departure from this threatens Europe with destabilization."[94] Soviet troops in the GDR were placed on a higher state of alert after reports that East German demonstrators were assembling around a Soviet base, although the Soviets assured the United States that it would not use force to reverse the changes occurring in East Germany.

The British Response

The British and French reactions were closer to that of the Soviet Union than to that of the United States. The British government saw in the fall of the Wall and the accelerating pace of unification a threat both to British sovereignty, which would result from attempts to speed up European integration as a means of containing the new Germany, and to its special relationship with the United States. As comments made by a close Thatcher associate, Nicholas Ridley, in the summer of 1990 confirmed, many in the Prime Minister's inner circle feared that a more integrated Europe would mean British subordination to the Germans.[95] The Prime Minister and her spokesmen began to speak of the need to "widen" the European Community to include Eastern Europe, opposing any new impetus to "deepen" the integration of the twelve member states first. Clearly the British government believed that widening would mean diluting European integration and thus reducing the threat to British sovereignty.[96]

In addition, German unification and Baker's talk of a new Atlanticism clearly implied a further downgrading of the special relationship between Great Britain and the United States and its replacement by a German-American partnership. Furthermore, it threatened to weaken NATO, the prime institutional link between Europe and the United States, a link in which the British could serve as a trans-Atlantic mediator, and replace it with a pan-European type of structure centered around the multinational Conference on Cooperation and Security in Europe (CSCE) where both American and British influence would be diminished.

Since the beginning of the Cold War, Germany had been the front line of British defense with about a third of the British Army and about half of the Royal Air Force based in the Federal Republic. The British government wanted united Germany to remain within NATO's integrated military structure to insure this front-line posture.

These fears were highlighted during the post-Malta NATO summit in early December when President Bush called for "intensified" movement toward EC integration, causing a widespread assumption in Britain that this was meant as a rebuke to Thatcher. During the Four Power talks in Berlin on December 11, Baker tried to soothe British sensibilities by reiterating, "Our relationship with Britain is extraordinarily special and will remain so."[97]

The British, like the other Allied Powers, were offended by Kohl's lack of consultation with them prior to the announcement of the Ten Point Plan and his failure to mention either NATO or the sanctity of the Polish-German border. Foreign Secretary Douglas Hurd responded to the plan by saying, "I think that we are pleased with the ten points. I believe that there is a need for an eleventh point which says that nothing will be done to destroy the balance and stability of Europe or create anxiety in the minds of people who have a right to be worried."[98]

Mrs. Thatcher called for existing borders to be undisturbed until democracy took deeper root, perhaps for 10 to 15 years. Throughout 1990 Thatcher consistently urged the Germans to have patience and not to rush unification. Yet the British were not able to argue openly against democratic self-determination and were increasingly pulled along by a desire not to become further isolated from the Americans.

In addition to concerns about the future of NATO and the impact of German unification upon the European Community, the United Kingdom was especially protective of its rights as a victor power in World War II. It viewed these as original rights stemming from its role in the victory over Germany in World War II and thus ones which could not be automatically erased by unification. They would, rather, have to be given up by each of the Four Powers voluntarily.[99]

The British view of developments in the early stages of unification differed sharply from those of the American Administration. The Thatcher Government was more skeptical about the chances of getting a unified Germany into NATO for a number of reasons. The German leaders tended to be talking more about CSCE in December and January than about NATO, with some even talking about a French-style membership for the new Germany in the Atlantic Alliance. As a leading British participant in the process later put it, "That kind of talk rattled us." The oscillating Soviet positions on the German question during the early months also made the British suspicious that the Soviets were trying to get a neutral Germany as the price for unification. As a result the British took the view early on that going slow on unification was more likely to keep Germany in NATO than the more rapid process favored by the Americans.[100]

The French Response

The French were the most disoriented by the changes which began with the opening of the Wall. While the French public was broadly supportive of German unification and felt it would help rather than hinder European integration, French leaders, like the British, feared they would be among the losers in the changes sweeping Europe.[101] The French image of Germany had been reshaped by generational change and by the daily experience of cooperation with the Germans fostered in part by an intensive exchange and information effort. Frenchmen and -women who were born after the war, consequently, were more positive in their views of Germany than were older generations.

Beginning in the early 1980s, French elites, especially within the intelligentsia, had begun to form a more suspicious and negative attitude toward West Germany. In the 1980s the "Gulag Effect" took hold among key segments of the intellectuals, most especially among the *nouveau philosphes*. These younger thinkers and opinion shapers had first reacted against communism in 1968 and then with great energy after the revelations of Aleksandr Solzhenitsyn in *The Gulag Archipelago*. The previous pro-Soviet and anti-American conventional wisdom of French intellectuals was shattered, especially among the generation of 1968.

At the same time, West Germany was going through détente and a mellowing of its concern about the Soviet Union and communism. Ostpolitik and the new dialogue with the GDR, combined with a critical distancing from the United States, set both German policymakers and intellectuals off in a direction in stark contrast to the trend in France. French writers, such as André Glucksman, were outraged by the rise of the peace movement in West Germany and saw in it the beginnings of neutralism and accommodation with the Soviets. These contrasts were paralleled by those in the political classes of the two countries. While the French left reaffirmed the centrality of nuclear deterrence under the Mitterrand Presidency, the German left and large elements of the right were questioning the viability and desirability of nuclear weapons.

The developments of late 1989 threatened the centrality of the French position in Europe and the credibility of its strategic doctrine. A unified Germany meant that France would lose the geographic buffer (or *glacis*) between itself and the East while facing a revived Germany that would have little need for U.S. forces and the restraints on German independence they implied. The new Germany would now be substantially larger in population than France and its already dominant economy would only become more so. Finally, a neutral or independent Germany would undermine the postwar balance of power under which France had been able to maintain its independent posture while assuring American engagement in the defense of Europe. It threatened, in the words of a French analyst, to "unhinge the balance between the French bomb and the German Mark and to destroy the prosperous stable club of the Europe of the Twelve."[102] The new Europe risked being dragged off by the Germans to the center of Europe, where the French were weakest. French elites came to believe that the division of Germany had enhanced the French role and that the end of this division meant the devaluation and vulnerability of France.[103]

This combination of geography and history made the French more pessimistic than the Americans about the pace and direction of German unification. While the Americans came to the conclusion "the sooner the better," the French were for a more cautious and incremental approach. They had been taken by surprise by the rapid rush of events in November and December. Reports from the French embassies in both Germanies did not reveal any belief that something big was about to happen.

Faced with the prospect of a diminished role and reduced independence in Europe it is not surprising that French leaders were unsure of what to do. They could not deny the democratic right of self-determination, nor could they afford to alienate their most important European ally, the Federal Republic, by opposing unification. They also lacked any real power to prevent unification if the Germans clearly wanted it. Yet they feared the consequences and were tempted to do what they could to stabilize the postwar system and the division of Germany.

Official French reaction to the developments of November and December were characterized, consequently, by attempts to slow down the pace of unification, to stabilize the GDR and to practice the traditional policy of *alliance de reverse* by reviving links to the Soviet Union and Poland. President Mitterrand had said only a week before the Wall opened, "I am not afraid of reunification," but while he accepted the German's right to self-determination, he emphasized that the rights of Germany's neighbors were also important. In other words, freedom was important but so was peace (that is, balance). President Mitterrand was closer to Thatcher than to Bush when he said that a vote by both Germanies to unite was "a necessary but not a sufficient condition" for German unity.[104]

Mitterrand was personally angered, as well, by Kohl's lack of consultation on the Ten Point Plan and by his ambiguity on the question of the Polish border. The French President had dined with the Chancellor on the Saturday before the plan was announced and was given no indication of Kohl's intentions. He saw this as both a personal affront and as a possible indicator of the future behavior of a new Germany. He warned that if the Germans were to give priority to unification over European integration then France would be free to create a new balance in Europe. Regis Debray, a Mitterrand advisor, wrote in an essay, "If a reunified Germany should develop too large a weight then one would have to retrieve the old Franco-Russian alliance from the mothballs."[105]

Immediately after Kohl's speech to the Bundestag, Mitterrand announced he would visit Modrow in December. He attempted to revive the relationship with Britain as well as hoped that the East Germans and the Soviets could prevent unification. Mitterrand flew to Kiev on December 6 for a meeting with Gorbachev where he made an attempt to get the Soviet leader to prevent unification. Gorbachev reportedly later related to Genscher that Mitterrand had asked him at Kiev to prevent unification.[106]

During his trip to the GDR on December 20 and 21, Mitterrand cautioned the East Germans against quick moves toward unification and discussed French cooperation with the SED. He toasted the "universal geniuses from *your* country, Bach, Händel, Luther, Nietzsche, Leibniz, Lessing," and assured Modrow, "You can count on the solidarity of France with the German Democratic Republic," adding with emphasis that there would be "both these German states."[107] He pointed out as well that the Four Powers retained certain responsibilities and thus "have their word to say." French behavior at the Berlin Four Power meeting was direct. When asked if Bonn would be displeased by the meeting, a senior French official replied, "That is the point of holding it."[108] Mitterrand became a vocal advocate for the Polish position on the inviolability of its western border.[109] The Brandenburg Gate opened during this visit but the French President decided not to accompany Kohl to this historically symbolic event.

These futile attempts at a policy, which irritated the Germans and caused strains in the close Franco-German relationship, continued until the decisive election in East Germany on March 18, 1990. It was only after those results and the settlement of the Polish border issue that the French President turned toward a more constructive diplomacy. Early French policy did have the intent, in the words of one of Genscher's close aides, of "showing the instruments of torture" the French had available to make life difficult for the Germans. However, Mitterrand soon took a more positive tack as he began to urge that the best response to the rapid unification he saw coming would be to accelerate the process of European integration. This period caused serious personal strains between Mitterrand and Kohl. The German Chancellor and his close advisors were angry and disappointed over the seeming irrelevance of years of close Franco-German cooperation to French policy in this period of great national hope for the Germans.

Throughout the 2 + 4 process the French, like the British, were more observers and critics than real participants. It wasn't until well into 1990 that the French were to begin to recover their balance while the British only made matters worse as the Thatcher era entered into its death throes. When the French reengaged, they chose the European Community, rather than the 2 + 4 talks, as the preferred arena for their actions. The 2 + 4 negotiations, after all, were a process dominated by the Anglo-Saxons and, like NATO, an instrument for American hegemony. It was useful only in so far as the French could protect their occupying rights in Berlin, but no further. The European Community, in contrast, was led by another French socialist, Jacques Delors, and was seen by the Mitterrand Government as a better vehicle for the creation of an independent Europe under French leadership.

4

Origins of 2 + 4

AVOIDING A NEW VERSAILLES

That the end of the division of Germany meant the end of the division of Europe was clear to everyone. What would follow was not. The 2 + 4 framework was established to fit the new Germany into the new Europe that its unification both symbolized and finalized.

The key issues for the 2 + 4 talks were those associated with creating what came to be called "the new European security architecture." The unification of Europe and of Germany was the direct result of the collapse of Soviet power or at least of the will of the Soviet leadership to exercise that power in the old imperial form. Yet it was in the interests of all concerned that this collapse be managed in a way that would create a new European political and security order that was acceptable to the key players. To be successful, 2 + 4 could not be seen as producing any losers.

As in the immediate postwar period, the Versailles analogy loomed over the talks in a variety of ways. A new Versailles that created a revisionist power determined in the future to forcibly reshape the European system (as did Nazi Germany in the 1930s) had to be precluded. The legitimate security interests of the Soviet Union, consequently, had to be taken into account in the settlement both because of continuing Soviet military power and to minimize the possibility that a future Soviet or Russian leadership might feel its interests were not secured in the new order and thus over-throw it. Also important was a Western desire to "help Gorbachev" so that he could have a settlement he could sell at home and that would allow him to continue his policies of perestroika and "new thinking." Off the record, James Baker bluntly referred to this as "giving cover" to the Soviets on German unification.[110]

Another aspect of the Versailles syndrome was a desire to meet the legitimate national interests of the new Germany and its neighbors, especially regarding the stability of borders and of the German military role in a new Europe. While losing the dubious merits of Soviet military protection, Central Europe wanted to insure that a new predator did not replace the old. The region did not want to revert to the position it had held during the interwar period, hanging precariously between Germany and the Soviet Union with no real security structure or guarantees. Poland was the key state regarding this dimension and played a side role in the talks. The talks also had to produce a result that a new sovereign Germany would accept as being legitimate and serving its fundamental interests. German power was rising as rapidly as Soviet power was declining and it was crucial that the new Germany be a "satisfied" or status quo power in the new Europe.

The stabilizing role of the United States in Europe had to be maintained. Everyone involved wanted to avoid the isolation of the United States from European affairs that had marked the interwar period and contributed to the destruction of the Versailles system and the war that followed. The United States must, in the words of George Bush, "remain a European power," yet one whose role was acceptable to both the Germans and the Russians.

Finally, these complicated international negotiations had to reach closure quickly enough to keep abreast with the accelerating dynamic of unification being generated within the two Germanies and to forestall an independent German path to unity. It is an intriguing aspect of this period that the actors involved returned to the interwar period as their historical reference point for shaping post-Cold War Europe. They seemed to sense that the end of the division of Europe would open up many of the problems which confronted the Continent in the 1920s and 1930s.

SEARCHING FOR A GRAND COMPROMISE: THE GENSCHER PLAN

By the beginning of 1990 the task for American and German diplomacy had become one of shaping an external framework for German unity. From the American perspective, a way had to be found to keep united Germany within NATO while at the same time reassuring the Soviets and building with them a new, more cooperative relationship. The Soviets had to be forced to deal constructively with what was for them the unpleasant prospect of "losing Germany" to the West. And the Germans had to be reminded to consider the interests of the other European nations and avoid the temptation of going it alone in shaping their new nation.[111] In this regard the United States needed to find a means to facilitate close consultation between the Germans and the Western allies. The United States, in the words of a State Department aide closely involved in the process, wanted to "avoid a one plus one," a German-Soviet deal taken without close consultation with the West. Additionally, the United States wished to bring along the East Germans, whose leaders and public were strongly neutralist, and convince them of the desirability of a NATO solution.

The key elements of the American approach to German unity in 1990, therefore, were first the principles laid down by George Bush and Baker in December, and in particular Baker's support for the CSCE as a way of giving the Soviets a place in the new Europe; second, the 2 + 4 mechanism, which provided separate fora for the internal and external aspects of unification; third, a modified Genscher Plan; fourth, the Nine Assurances offered at the Washington Soviet-American summit in May-June; and, finally, the NATO London declaration of July. All of these elements will be discussed fully later in this study.

These elements were all linked inextricably to the future security status of unified Germany. Once a security status for the new Germany could be created that respected the vital security interests of the key parties then the rest would be minor details. The Genscher Plan was to provide a key to the solution of this problem.

By the end of 1989, Helmut Kohl was still working on the assumption that unification was three to four years away and it seemed that the two Germanies could coexist for some time in a cooperative relationship. The situation in the GDR, however, continued to deteriorate and to undermine any outside attempts to consolidate the two countries. Even by the end of November, Wolfgang Berghofer, the mayor of Dresden and a leading SED reformer, was saying, "The people have taken power away from us. The leading role of the SED is fundamentally already history."[112]

The root causes of the destabilization of the East German state lay in the realization that the Soviets would not act to save it from the lack of any credible political alternative in the GDR. The Modrow Government made one last attempt to save the communist state by attempting to restore the control of the Stasi through reorganization. On January 3, a number of Soviet war memorials were defaced and splattered with extreme right-wing slogans. It is most likely that Stasi agents were responsible for these provocations but the Modrow Government, under intense pressure from the Stasi, blamed them on right-wing extremist groups and attempted to use the incidents to revive the secret police as a new "constitutional protection force." On January 8, an opposition roundtable protested this restoration, and on January 15, large demonstrations erupted, resulting in the sacking of the Stasi central headquarters in East Berlin. The West German parties all agreed to withhold any community of treaties until the GDR held free elections. The economy was reeling and emigration of East Germans into West Germany was running at a rate of between 40,000 and 50,000 per month.

On January 28, Modrow agreed with the opposition roundtable to form a "government of national responsibility" and to move the date for the parliamentary elections planned for May 6 up to March 18. Hans Modrow traveled to Moscow on January 30 for a meeting with Mikhail Gorbachev. After the meeting Gorbachev stated that the Soviet Union did not object to German unification in principle and that "no one had ever cast doubt on the unification of the Germans." On February 1, the desperate Modrow announced his "Declaration on the Way to German Unity," which he had worked out with Gorbachev. The Modrow plan proposed a confederation of the two German states, which would lead to a federation, and both German states would move step by step away from their alliance commitments and toward a neutral military status.

This marked the end of the first stage in the history of the diplomacy of German unification. A fundamentally new situation existed that required a means for structuring the order that would follow the one that was dying. By this point, Kohl had decided that unity was going to come faster than he had thought only a few weeks earlier. The Ten Point Plan, which had looked so bold in November, was now clearly obsolete. Discussions began in the first week of February on the introduction of the Deutsche Mark into East Germany. The West German Chancellor welcomed Modrow's acceptance of a single German state but rejected any neutral status for a unified Germany, arguing that it would contradict the process of a pan-European unification process.

It was at this stage, as one analyst observed later, "when any serious Soviet bid to veto NATO membership for a united Germany might well have succeeded."[113] Unification euphoria was still high in both Germanies, and public support for NATO was fragile and could have collapsed if it were seen as standing in the way of unification and the withdrawal of foreign troops. Many, both in West Germany and in the West in general, were worried that a referendum on NATO might be called with negative results.

The Genscher Plan was developed during this period by the West German Foreign Minister as a means of selling unification to the Soviets without paying the price of leaving NATO. Ideas about limiting the extension of NATO into the territory of what would be the former GDR had been circulating among sources as diverse as the Hessian Institute for Peace

Research and Horst Teltschik. Some even pointed to Adenauer and his ideas about a demilitarized GDR in the 1950s.[114] Key Foreign Ministry aides were already discussing aspects of what became the plan in late December, informing visitors at the time that Kohl's ideas about confederation were not realistic because the forces moving toward unification were too strong.

Hans-Dietrich Genscher, with his astute sense of tactics, seized upon these ideas in late January as a way out of the box in which the German leaders had found themselves. Genscher was sensitive to Gorbachev's need not to be humiliated by German unification and to avoid an outcome that would make the Soviet Union look as if it had lost the Cold War. At the same time, Genscher was convinced that German unification had to occur within a larger framework of European integration (creating a European Germany, not a German Europe) and along terms that were acceptable to the Americans. Baker had stated in his Berlin speech that German unity must be accomplished without sacrificing the future of NATO.

The final compromise had to include maintaining NATO in a form that would not be seen by the Soviets as detrimental to their vital security interests and prestige. Giving up the great prize of World War II was difficult enough for Soviets of the generation which fought in the "great patriotic war," yet accepting the accession of Moscow's most vital and reliable military ally in the Warsaw Pact into NATO was rubbing salt in the wound.

The Genscher Plan was designed to assuage these Soviet concerns by assuring the Soviet Union that the GDR would not become a platform for NATO forces and at the same time offering a new "kinder, gentler" NATO that would move from being an alliance that confronted the Soviets to one that could serve as a vehicle for cooperative security. Genscher worked out his approach with his key advisors and then began to articulate it prior to the pivotal Kohl-Genscher-Gorbachev meeting in Moscow on February 10.

Through a series of newspaper interviews and a speech delivered to a conference held at the Tutzing Protestant Academy on January 31, the Foreign Minister presented his grand compromise on NATO and German unity.[115] In his Tutzing speech, Genscher forcefully restated the German commitment to developing German unity within a European framework, what he called the "Germans' European vocation." Unity must mean a declaration guaranteeing the frontiers of all of Germany's neighbors. German membership in the European Community and NATO must remain "irrevocable." "We do not want a united neutralist Germany." At the same time, he clearly gave priority to the European Community and the CSCE as the frameworks for a new European security order.

He then turned to the need to give special attention to the security interests of the Soviet Union, given the deterioration of COMECON and the Warsaw Pact.

> What NATO must do is state unequivocally that whatever happens in the Warsaw Pact there will be no expansion of NATO territory eastwards, that is to say closer to the borders of the Soviet Union. . . .
>
> Any proposals for incorporating the part of Germany at present forming the GDR in NATO's military structures would block intra-German rapprochement. The important thing is to clearly define the future role of the two alliances. They will move away from confrontation towards cooperation and will become elements of cooperative security structures throughout Europe.[116]

The Foreign Minister's remarks met initial acceptance from within the CDU, at least as voiced by the party's Secretary General, Volker Rühe. The issue was, however, to reemerge after the Kohl-Genscher meeting with Gorbachev in the middle of February.[117] (The development of the final agreement on the nature of military deployments in the former GDR and the size of the limits on the Bundeswehr is discussed in Chapter 7).

THE ORIGINS OF 2 + 4

By the end of January, at about the same time Helmut Kohl came to the same belief, the Bush Administration concluded that the GDR was collapsing and that German unity was now a certainty, and should be accelerated. President Bush consulted with Brent Scowcroft and Scowcroft's deputy, Robert Gates, while Baker worked with Robert Zoellick, Dennis Ross and Raymond Seitz, the Assistant Secretary of State for European Affairs, on a plan to manage unification. Zoellick and Ross wrote for Baker a plan widely referred to within the Administration as "2 + 4."

The two Baker aides had been thinking about the need to manage the external aspects of unification. While the two German states could manage internal unification on their own, the diplomatic side was not as simple. A Four Power framework would not work because it excluded the Germans. NATO was too big and therefore unwieldy, as was the CSCE. Ross and Zoellick thus seized upon an idea, which had originated within the Policy Planning staff, of 2 + 4 (the two Germanies plus the Four Powers), with a clear emphasis on the two preceding the four.

They knew it would be controversial because it might be seen as an intervention of the Four Powers in German affairs, something the Administration had rejected early on but was sensitive to because of the Soviet attempts to use the Four Power meeting in Berlin in December for this purpose. In order to avoid having the plan be seen as a contradiction to this policy, Ross and Zoellick made it clear that a precondition for 2 + 4 negotiations must be that its explicit objective was a unified Germany. Everyone involved had to sign off on this or there would be no negotiation under the 2 + 4 framework. In order to shelter internal unification from the external process, they stated that the plan would not go into operation until after the March 18 election in the GDR and after the start of German-German negotiations for unity.

Both Zoellick and Ross knew that by proposing this plan they were endorsing rapid unification. The 2 + 4 framework would be, in the words of a National Security Council aide, "a means of managing Soviet concerns. Some within the U.S. government were opposed on the grounds that this would throw the Soviets a life-line at a time when the West should take advantage of Soviet weakness."[118] The NSC in particular was concerned that this mechanism would allow the Soviets to obstruct German unification, a point that did not impress Zoellick, who argued that the presence of 380,000 Soviet troops in the GDR was means enough for obstruction.

Baker agreed with the formula and presented it in an abbreviated form to British Foreign Secretary Douglas Hurd on January 29 in Washington. Hurd responded that Britain preferred a "4 + 0" approach, in which the Four Powers would agree on an approach without Germany, but he acquiesced to the 2 + 4 framework.[119]

Genscher flew to Washington for talks with Baker on February 2 to test the American response to his proposal on the future military status of the GDR. He was preceded by his personal assistant, Frank Elbe, who had discussed the plan with Zoellick and Ross. Zoellick agreed that it was a good way out of the NATO dilemma but added that a mechanism was needed which included all the six. He laid the 2 + 4 plan out to Elbe, who reacted positively to what Zoellick proposed.

Elbe then went to meet Genscher and Dieter Kastrup, Political Director of the Foreign Ministry, at the airport and briefed them on the drive into town. He told them that the United States agreed with the Tutzing thinking, and when he raised Zoellick's idea of the mechanism of the six, Genscher agreed with it. Upon his arrival at the State Department that evening, Genscher went directly to the Secretary's office, where he and Baker took off their jackets, sat in front of the fireplace and discussed the plan. At the conclusion of their conversation, the two men agreed on both the Tutzing outline and the mechanism of six. They called their aides into the office to announce their accord. President Bush publicly greeted the Genscher Plan at a press conference in San Francisco, saying, "When I hear Mr. Genscher and Chancellor Kohl talk about a Germany that in some way remains a part of NATO—perhaps not a NATO in the exact same form as it exists today—then I am encouraged."[120] Again the Versailles analogy was working, as both Baker and Genscher were sensitive to Gorbachev's need to sell an agreement to his party and his military.

Baker and his aides, while generally supportive of the Genscher Plan, were concerned about some of its ambiguities. The Americans felt that the plan had not been thought through and wanted clarification on such points as the role of NATO structures in the former East Germany and particularly the role of the Bundeswehr in the East, especially as the plan did not include any provision for Bundeswehr forces to be stationed in the former GDR. The Americans also pressed for the possibility of NATO forces in eastern Germany and expressed the desire to avoid making the eastern region of Germany a demilitarized zone. Genscher countered that NATO defense commitments would not extend to the territory of the GDR. This was, in the view of one of the Americans involved, a proposal to "neutralize" the GDR.[121] A number of Americans were concerned that if the Germans were to change their mind in the future about the need to send forces into eastern Germany, a repeat of the Rheinland experience of the 1930s could result. President Bush was adamant that all Soviet forces be out of eastern Germany within three to four years. This was faster than Genscher thought was acceptable to the Soviets. Baker, however, did not immediately pick up on the implications of what Genscher was proposing during their meeting.

At the same time, the Americans shared Genscher's desire to avoid creating a crisis for Gorbachev. Baker agreed to a summit conference of the CSCE states later in the year with the condition that there was a prior agreement on conventional forces in Europe (CFE). The Americans, however, were determined not to involve CSCE in German unification because they felt that, with its thirty-five member states, it would be too unwieldy.

Genscher accepted the approach because it avoided what the Germans most wanted to avoid: a larger peace conference leading to a peace treaty. He wanted to keep out additional players, who could raise claims for reparations and other complications. As a number of those Germans involved put it later, "We wanted to keep out those like Argentina which declared war at the end of WWII but might raise claims as a victor power."[122]

In the days that followed the meeting, the National Security Council staff and the State Department began to focus on the Genscher Plan and to worry about its "neutralization" aspects. A visit by the Secretary General of NATO and the former West German Minister of Defense, Manfred Wörner, to

Washington during these days proved felicitous. Wörner used the term "special military status" in referring to the GDR territory in a meeting with Bush, and the NSC staff put this phrase into a letter from the President to Kohl.

Baker then flew to Moscow, securing French Foreign Minister Roland Dumas's agreement at Shannon Airport en route, although Dumas, like Hurd, preferred the 4 + 0 approach. Baker briefed reporters on the plane on the details of the compromise that had emerged, labeling it the Genscher Plan. In Moscow on February 8, Baker raised the idea with Gorbachev, who remained noncommittal but also clearly preferred 4 + 0. Baker then turned to the question of the membership of united Germany in NATO. He asked the Soviet leader, "Would you prefer to see a united Germany outside of NATO and with no U.S. forces, or would you prefer to see a united Germany tied to NATO, with assurances that NATO's jurisdiction would not shift one inch eastward from its present position?"[123] Gorbachev responded that any extension of NATO would be unacceptable but that NATO membership for Germany within its existing borders might be acceptable. While he was keeping his options open, he stressed the depth of opposition within his country to German unification.

Baker, however, sold the idea of 2 + 4 to Shevardnadze. When the Soviet Foreign Minister was asked about the plan by *Newsweek* correspondent Margaret Warner he replied that he thought that Genscher had said many reasonable things, including those things he had said in the Plan. Baker passed on Gorbachev's reaction via an "eyes only" memo to Kohl, who had just arrived in Moscow. In the memo the Secretary wrote,

> Gorbachev at least is not locked in. While he has real concerns about German unification—some of which may be related to the passions this issue evokes in the Soviet Union—he may be willing to go along with a sensible approach that gives him some cover or explanation of his actions.

> I suspect that the combination of Two Plus Four mechanism and a broader CSCE framework might do that. But it is obviously too early to know, and we'll have to see how the Soviet position evolves.[124]

During these meetings in Moscow, Baker, for the first time, presented what came to be known as the Nine Assurances. These assurances, already out in public in various proposals, concerned what the West could offer to the Soviet Union in return for acceptance of German unification. Robert Zoellick put them into one package of cooperative measures that were restated throughout the following months (most explicitly during the May summit in Washington, where they were described more fully). The American message was, in the words of a senior State Department official involved, "Here is what we can do for you. But you can't wait and we can't wait long because the internal dynamic of unification is moving too fast. No one can leave you out except yourselves."[125]

At a press conference held at the conclusion of his visit, Baker stated that "the United States does not favor neutrality for a unified Germany; that we favor continued membership in *or association with* [author's italics] NATO; and that we feel that there should be no extension of NATO forces eastward in order to assuage the security concerns of those east of Germany."[126] The phrase "association" was a misstatement that Baker corrected a few minutes later when he said that "the preferred position of the United States is that Germany retain its membership in NATO." He went on to add that NATO would change its character to become less of a security alliance and more of a political alliance. He added, "I don't mean to send any signal that we're in any way changing that aspect of our position regarding German reunification." He came back at the end of the press conference to refer to "some chance that there would be some special arrangements within NATO respecting the extension of NATO forces eastward."

SECURING THE KEY TO GERMAN UNITY

Prior to Kohl's departure for Moscow he received what Administration sources called "a very important" letter, in which Bush spelled out what the Soviets could do to the Germans, or threaten to do, and what the United States could do for Germany to counter any anticipated Soviet actions. The letter was, in the American view, crucial to bolster Kohl for a visit that Bush described as the most important trip to the Soviet Union by a West German Chancellor since Adenauer's in 1955, the first such visit by a West German leader and one that secured the release of German prisoners of war.

Kohl's talks with Gorbachev bore out this prophecy. He and Genscher had intensive discussions with the Soviet leader and Shevardnadze on security arrangements. Shevardnadze reported on the criticism of Gorbachev's foreign policy voiced in the recent session of the Central Committee. Numerous speakers, he said, had attacked the leadership for the neglect of Soviet security interests, asking, "What are you doing with our security?"[127] On the key question of alliance membership, Shevardnadze said that the neutralization of Germany was a "good old idea" of Moscow's from the 1950s, but was open to other variations. Kohl, however, was clear with Gorbachev that a neutral Germany "is not a question for us" and that

Germany would remain part of NATO.[128] The German leaders presented the Genscher Plan as a means of making this provision acceptable to the Soviet Union. In a confidential West German government report on the visit, Genscher was reported to believe that the issue of the orderly withdrawal of Soviet forces was crucial because "for the Soviets it is not only a question of security but a problem of keeping face with their own people."[129]

According to the West German official account, Kohl then turned to the economic advantages of unification for the Soviets. He described the catastrophic condition of the East German economy to the Soviet leaders, and Gorbachev replied that Bonn would free Moscow of this burden by taking over responsibility for the GDR. This stabilization, the Soviet leader added, was of interest as well because of the presence of Soviet troops in the GDR. "Because of the daily disintegration of the GDR," he said, "it is now inevitable that the two German states come to an agreement on the most compatible way to unity."[130]

Genscher assured the Soviet leader that the borders of the new Germany would comprise the territory of the Federal Republic, the GDR and Berlin, "not less, but not more." The Germans agreed to pick up the export obligations of East Germany to the Soviet Union after unification and to assist the Soviet economy with immediate shipments of meat, butter and cheese.

At the conclusion of the meeting Gorbachev grasped both of Genscher's hands and said, "We must do all of this very cautiously." Genscher replied with a reference to his roots in Halle: "I understand. You know where I come from and what this means."[131] Kohl came away with what he described as "the key to German unity." The Chancellor, in his statement at the conclusion of the talks, said,

> General Secretary Gorbachev and I agree that it is the right of the German people alone to decide whether they want to live in one state.
>
> General Secretary Gorbachev promised me in no uncertain terms that the Soviet Union will respect the Germans' decision to live in one state, and that it is up to the Germans themselves to determine the time of unification and the way it will come about. . . . [We] also agreed that the German question can only be solved on the basis of realities; that means that it must be embedded in the pan-European architecture and in the general process of East-West relations. . . .
>
> Ladies and gentlemen, this is a good day for Germany, and a happy day for me personally.[132]

After the Moscow meeting Kohl opened up a bottle of champagne. The Germans present felt the deal was done in principle. Teltschik declared a week later that the GDR stood on the brink of bankruptcy and that the key to German unity no longer lay in Moscow. "The Chancellor has retrieved the key. It is now in Bonn."[133]

However, while Gorbachev accepted that internal unification was a matter for the Germans, he made it clear that the external aspects were far from an exclusively German affair. He stated that solution of the German question was "inseparable" from disarmament in Europe and had to occur only with the acceptance of the Four Powers.

AGREEMENT IN OTTAWA

Although Baker did not receive official Soviet acceptance of 2 + 4 in Moscow, the Kohl-Genscher-Gorbachev meeting set the stage for an agreement that came a few days later during the opening meeting of the "open skies" conference in Ottawa, Canada. The four Foreign Ministers spent much of the time in Ottawa conferring with each other, while President Bush, meanwhile, was telephoning Kohl to insure that the Chancellor would support what Genscher was agreeing to in Canada. Teltschik had phoned the White House during the Ottawa talks and left the impression with Scowcroft that the Chancellor did not support Genscher on the question of an international negotiation over German unity, reportedly because Teltschik feared that a 2 + 4 process would allow the Foreign Office to gain bureaucratic control over the question of German unity. This caused a good deal of anxiety within the NSC over the 2 + 4 idea.

During Ottawa, Baker told Genscher that Bush had doubts about the extent to which the Chancellor was supporting the line of his Foreign Minister. Genscher phoned the Chancellor and urged him to clarify his position with Bush, which he did.[134] The message, however, was not clearly understood within the NSC, and Kohl had to make yet another phone call to Bush to restate his support for the formula. Kohl was assured by the Americans that a division of labor would occur in which the Chancellor would manage internal unification and the Americans would handle the external aspects.

When Baker presented the Western proposal to the Soviet Foreign Minister, his reaction was not friendly. While Shevardnadze basically agreed with the plan, he felt things were moving too fast, responding that he would have to talk to his allies. Shevardnadze and Gorbachev finally agreed to holding a series of talks at the foreign minister level of the Four Powers and the two Germanies. They attached a proviso that no explicit link be made between the beginning of the talks and the March 18 elections in the GDR and that some reference be made to the security of neighboring states.

Once all the principals were in agreement, the announcement was made by the four Foreign Ministers to the surprise and anger of the Dutch, Italians and Belgians. As one American official recounted, "They were told in no uncertain terms that this was a matter for the Allied powers with legal rights in Germany and nobody else. That is why the deal was cut this way, we told them and if you don't like it, I'm sorry but you have no legal rights."[135] Genscher was more blunt, telling the Italian foreign minister, "You are not part of the game."[136] The Western Foreign Ministers also agreed not to extend NATO to the east and to let the Soviets know that the Western Alliance would not accept the former Warsaw Pact states as members in NATO.[137]

At the conclusion of the Ottawa meeting the major powers had reacted to the new situation created by the collapse of the German Democratic Republic with agreement for a framework shaping the Germany and Europe that would follow. The process had been established, but not the product. That would result from the negotiations that were now to follow and that would consume the next five months.

5

Negotiating German Unification: The Opening Phase

OBJECTIVES OF THE PLAYERS AT THE START OF 2 + 4

The third period in the history of the diplomacy of German unification now began, namely, the negotiation phase. This period can be divided into two subphases: the first, which ran from the end of February until early July, in which the preconditions for a final deal were established; and the second, in which the deal was closed, which ran from the Caucasus meeting until the signing of the final agreement in September.

The 2 + 4 process was influenced by two key factors that set the parameters for the final agreement. These were the growing perception of the rapid decline of Soviet power by all the players and conversely the recognition of the rise of German power. All six of the players were aware that the final settlement would, in fact, be shaped by the Soviets and the Germans, with the United States playing an important role as mediator. It was already clear in February that East Germany had ceased to be an independent actor, and after the March 18 elections it became a subsidiary of the CDU-led government in Bonn.

West Germany

West German objectives at the beginning of the negotiations were the rapid unification of the nation, the termination of allied rights in Germany and Berlin and the restoration of full sovereignty to Germany. Chancellor Helmut Kohl's greatest ambition was "that we become a wholly normal country."[138] Hans-Dietrich Genscher was saying the same thing. He told *Der Spiegel* in May, "We want German unity and as quickly as possible and we want the same sovereignty which the other states in Europe also have."[139] The new

Germany that would emerge must be treated as a normal European nation and not as a defeated power. For this reason the talks should not conclude in a peace treaty but rather in an all-European CSCE conference that would ratify the restoration of German sovereignty. Throughout, the West Germans insisted on referring to 2 + 4 as a consultative process and wished to avoid any hint of receiving terms from the Four Powers.

Within this broad objective were a number of more specific goals. In Genscher's words, the new Germany was to consist of the two German states and Berlin—"nothing more and nothing less." The German government never made any claim to former German territories in Poland and the Soviet Union, but at the outset of the talks there was a disagreement over how and when to make this clear. In particular, there was disagreement within the West German government about whether the parliament of a unified Germany should finally and legally renounce such claims or whether this should be done by West Germany prior to unification. This conflict is treated in detail later in this chapter.

In addition, the West German government wished to avoid any re-opening of claims for reparations. By early 1990, the FRG had been approached by representatives of the Yugoslav and Romanian governments with requests to discuss reparations. While the government was divided over the question of the claims of individuals for restitution of lost property, there was a consensus that national requests for reparations had to be rejected. Germany had over 40 official enemies by the end of World War II, and the FRG had already made substantial payments to the Four Powers, Israel and Poland.[140]

The West Germans wished to unify their country within a stable European framework. This meant not only satisfying what they considered to be the legitimate security concerns of the Soviet Union but also having the sovereign right to choose their own international alliances and commitments, in effect remaining a member of the transformed NATO that was a factor in the creation of cooperative security structures in Europe. The Germans were willing to reduce the size of their own defense forces so long as Germany was not "singularized" for special treatment. Thus, any reductions would have to be part of a general European agreement that limited the forces of the other nations as well. The German government, however, wanted to keep such types of questions out of the 2 + 4 process and include them, instead, within CFE and other arms control negotiations.[141]

The Soviet Union

The objectives of the Soviet Union at the outset were shaped by the interplay between Mikhail Gorbachev's need to maintain domestic support for his policies while allowing the "prize" of World War II to slip away. Gorbachev had to concede that which he no longer could hold at an acceptable cost and come out of the process with a settlement that he could sell to his military as not detrimental to Soviet security and that provided external support for restructuring the Soviet economy.

Although numerous Soviet spokesmen had raised the objective of German neutrality,[142] the Soviets had probably given up on the possibility or even the desirability of a neutral Germany by the start of the 2 + 4 negotiations. As one of Genscher's advisors stated in February, "Gorbachev is a realist who knows that today neutrality is no longer to be had."[143] The Soviet Union's Warsaw Pact allies were openly stating that they wished to see a united Germany remain embedded in NATO, and Vyacheslav Dashichev had written a famous memo in 1990 arguing that a neutralized united Germany made no sense.[144]

The Soviet government wished to see a reduced German military that remained nonnuclear. Their goal was a Bundeswehr of 200,000 and a Soviet presence in Germany of 20,000 to 50,000, both by the end of three to five years. U.S. forces in Germany could remain higher. Ultimately all Soviet forces would be withdrawn from Germany. German membership in NATO might continue but in an altered form, perhaps along the lines of French membership. Gorbachev had spoken with Hans Modrow about a Germany that belonged to both alliances. The Soviet objective was to alter the status of West Germany "in order that it is no longer positioned as the strategic and geographic crux of the NATO alliance."[145]

The economic aspects of 2 + 4 were as important as the military aspects to the Soviets. A united Germany would have to assume all the obligations of the former GDR to COMECON countries and the COCOM list would have to be shortened to allow greater Soviet access to West German technology.

The Soviets also stressed the need for agreements that would provide maximum security for the existing borders of European states, probably through a series of bilateral agreements between the Germans and their neighbors. Some Soviet officials left open the question of reparations and restitution.

The United States

The United States entered the 2 + 4 process with the general objective of achieving complete sovereignty for a unified Germany while maintaining a stable West European security system with a strong American role. NATO was seen by the key American players as the sine qua non for a stable Europe. The United States not only wanted a unified Germany within NATO but also a NATO that remained a meaningful military alliance with an integrated command structure.

By February Washington had come to the view that 2 + 4 should deal with ending the semi-sovereignty of Germany and not with resolving major security issues. The negotiations were, in the words of a senior State Department official, the center ring of a "multiple ring circus," which would act as a steering group referring issues to the appropriate forum rather than as a decision group that would solve everything.[146] Once sovereign, Germany would have the right to decide to which alliances it wished to adhere. Arms control and other security-related aspects of this new nation would be dealt with in other arenas, such as the CFE talks and CSCE. The future of nuclear weapons in Germany was a NATO and a bilateral matter and not one for 2 + 4.[147]

Beyond the essentiality of NATO, the United States wanted the border issue with Poland resolved and supported Polish participation during the portion of the 2 + 4 talks that dealt with the issue. Most American officials at the time believed that a treaty would be required between Poland and Germany that permanently fixed the Oder-Neisse line as the final border. The United States was not interested in reparations, although it insisted that individual claims by Americans whose property had been expropriated, claims valued at $78 million, would have to be addressed by a unified German government.

The United States had no desire to retain any of its rights as a victor power and desired the abrogation of Four Power rights in Berlin and the rest of Germany as quickly as possible. The Bush Administration did not wish to remove American forces from Berlin so long as Soviet forces remained in the country, but wished U.S. forces to remain in Berlin on the basis of a bilateral agreement with Germany.

France and Britain

The positions of the other two powers were generally similar to those of the United States. They wished to move expeditiously to terminate Four Power rights while keeping forces on a bilateral basis in Berlin for as long as Soviet

forces remained in the country. Both were strong supporters of the inviolability of the current German-Polish border and wished to have the border
issue settled in a legally binding document. The British wanted 2 + 4 to do
more than just bring Four Power rights to an end in Germany. They also
wanted the negotiating process to deal with the implications of unification
for NATO, CSCE and other contextual aspects. While the British supported
the American view on the importance of a united Germany's staying in
NATO, the French stressed more the significance of CSCE and the EC.

Neither Britain or France had any interest in reparations. However, both
were more insistent than the Americans about obtaining a legally binding
document that would be the equivalent of a peace treaty. The British
delegation, in particular, was staffed with legal experts and was especially
punctilious on the legal questions.

The Western powers agreed that the talks should be about finishing the
unfinished business of Potsdam and settling the status of Berlin. They wanted
the task of laying foundations for a new security arrangement for Europe to
be undertaken outside of the 2 + 4 talks. They wished to insure only that the
process not jeopardize the prospects for a new stable security system. The
Soviets, by contrast, were interested in putting as much of the new security
arrangements as possible into 2 + 4.

Given these divergent starting positions it became clear that the main
objective of the talks was to convince the Soviets to accept a sovereign
Germany within NATO and to elicit from the Germans a clear binding
agreement on the permanence of their borders. The four formal 2 + 4
ministerial-level meetings that occurred between May and September (held
in Bonn, Berlin, Paris and Moscow) merely registered the results of an
intensive series of bilateral meetings and a large number of lower-level
meetings.

Especially significant were what American participants dubbed the 1 + 3
talks, held among the political directors of the four Western Foreign Offices.
This to many was the most important level of the entire 2 + 4 process because
it was here that the Western allies worked out the positions they would take
in their meetings with the Soviets. They served another important function
by clarifying to the West Germans what agreements their allies would find
acceptable in German negotiations with the Soviets. In the words of an
American participant, the 1 + 3 "prevented Genscher from cutting a quick
deal," a comment which reflected suspicion within the NSC staff about the
German Foreign Minister.[148] The Americans tended to view this process as
critical although not visible to many outside observers.

With the German assurances to the Americans about NATO confirmed, 2 + 4 rapidly became a German-Soviet dialogue with the United States acting to facilitate matters, although the Americans saw their role as bolstering the Western position with Bonn. The United States continually reassured the Soviets that accepting a unified Germany within NATO would not threaten but actually promote their vital security interests. The U.S. side was convinced from the beginning of 2 + 4 that the Soviets would come around, although it would take time.

The Soviets were not in a strong position as they were left with the diminishing leverage of their 380,000 troops in the GDR and little else. They could hope to play on Kohl's increasingly obvious desire to gain rapid unification to exact the best price possible, but they could no longer credibly threaten to halt the process toward unification. The costs looked too great to be acceptable. Gorbachev's position at home was deteriorating day by day: He was faced with nationality challenges in the Baltic states and much of the western Soviet Union and the Soviet economy was falling into a tailspin.

RESOLVING POLAND'S BORDER: CAMP DAVID AND BEYOND

Throughout the eleven months from the opening of the Wall to the unification of Germany, Chancellor Kohl had an unerring touch. His handling of the Polish border issue, however, may have been an exception, as he appeared to many to be holding this essentially closed issue open for much too long. While the vast majority of Germans in both Germanies, including Genscher and most of the West German establishment, as well as all the governments in the 2 + 4 believed that the Oder-Neisse border was a closed question and should be legally recognized as such, Kohl held the position that only an all-German government could formally renounce any change in the postwar German border.

The Polish border thus became the most divisive issue within the Bonn coalition. Just prior to Kohl's November visit to Poland, which was interrupted by the opening of the Berlin Wall, Genscher had declared that the Polish people should know that "their right to live in secure borders will neither now nor in the future be put in question by us Germans through territorial claims."[149] The gap between Kohl and Genscher widened on November 8, 1989, when the Bundestag passed a resolution affirming that the West German government would not try to revise the Oder-Neisse border. While Genscher wanted to settle the issue immediately, Kohl was more wary about early closure. Besides the legal question over whether a West German government could speak for a united Germany, Kohl and his advisers were concerned about a possible peace treaty rather than a settlement. The issue of reparation demands was very much in the Chancellor's mind when he dealt with the Polish border resolution. He wished to achieve a quick, overall, one-package agreement rather than settling issues individually in prolonged negotiations that would end up in an ever expanding series of claims from numerous countries.

Kohl's hesitation also came from his desire to avoid alienating those Germans who were forcibly expelled from what had once been German territory and was now Poland. These groups were strong supporters of the CDU and the CSU and thus presented Kohl with a problem neither Genscher nor the SPD faced, a problem heightened by the Republikaner party challenge to the right of the Union parties. The Republikaner had shocked the CDU and especially the CSU leadership with its strong electoral showing in a series of elections in 1989 in Berlin and Hesse as well as in the European parliamentary election. They were especially strong in Bavaria, receiving up to a quarter of the vote in some constituencies. In addition, Kohl was facing an election on March 18 in the GDR in which his Christian Democratic allies were thought to be trailing the SPD. He was sensitive to the strong anti-Polish sentiment of many East Germans and did not wish to alienate these new voters as well. Finally, he wished to keep the issue in reserve to offer the Soviets as part of the price he would pay for a final agreement.

While Kohl knew that the border issue was closed, he wanted to be seen as having been pushed reluctantly into accepting it, thus holding on to this element of his constituency and accepting some limited political fallout. Genscher and the Free Democrats, always looking for an issue to use as evidence of their role as a moderating factor in German politics, seized upon the Polish border controversy with alacrity. Kohl's reluctance also revived foreign concerns about the behavior of a future unified Germany. It put pressure on President Bush to get a firm commitment from the German Chancellor when they met at Camp David for two days of talks on February 24 and 25.

The U.S. government was divided over how to handle the border issue. While the Policy Planning Staff was urging strong American pressure on Kohl to accede, the NSC staff, Embassy Bonn and the European Bureau did not want the United States to be seen as pressuring the Chancellor. The State Department's Legal Bureau took the view that Kohl's position on the border issue was not a legally sound one. He could, in the view of the lawyers, make a declaration that would have the force of a treaty with Poland and simply reassert it after German unification.

When all was said and done, "the Polish border was small potatoes" to the United States, in the view of one of the lawyers involved in the discussions. The Administration was not very supportive of the Polish demands, believing that it was up to the Germans to work out a settlement and being intent on avoiding a creation of a 2 + 5 process. There was, perhaps surprisingly, little reported pressure on U.S. policymakers by Polish-American groups.

At Camp David, Bush and Kohl openly disagreed on the Polish border issue. At a press conference held at the conclusion of the talks, Kohl stated that while "no one has any intention of linking the questions of national unity to the change of existing borders," only a freely elected all-German parliament could as a "legally competent sovereign" make a final decision on the matter. He added, "I think we have learned lessons and we do not want to repeat the errors of history." Bush pointedly responded, "The U.S. respects the provisions of the Helsinki Final Act regarding the inviolability of current borders in Europe, and the U.S. formally recognizes the current German-Polish border."[150] The President spoke of an "alignment" rather than an agreement of U.S. and German positions on this issue.

Soon after returning from Camp David, the Chancellor proposed a guarantee of the Polish border by both German parliaments after the March 18 election in the GDR on the condition that Poland renounce all claims to World War II reparations and guarantee the rights of the German minority remaining in Poland. He made this controversial linkage between the border resolution and reparations after discussing it with a small group in the Chancellory but without consulting the Foreign Minister, who had not accompanied the Chancellor to Camp David.[151]

Kohl's stand at Camp David and afterward increased the pressures both from within and outside of Germany. Genscher and the head of the FDP, Graf Otto von Lambsdorff, raised the issue to a crisis in the first week of March, suggesting that the coalition might break up over it. The French Foreign Minister, Roland Dumas, made strong statements on the need to reaffirm the border, and President Mitterrand warmly received President Wojciech Jaruzelski of Poland and his Solidarity-supported Prime Minister, Tadeusz Mazowiecki, in Paris on March 8.

The crisis was resolved when the cabinet decided to accept Genscher's position and agreed that both German parliaments would declare the inviolability of the Polish border as soon as possible after the March 18 election and that the issue would be settled in a German-Polish treaty soon after unification. The cabinet also agreed to Polish representation at the 2 + 4 talks when issues affecting Poland were discussed.[152] The Chancellor issued a statement that "mistakes were made on all sides, also by me," referring to his linkage of the border issue with the renunciation of reparations.

Having offered his own display of resistance while demonstrating the foreign opposition to any revision of the border and at the same time seizing the reunification issue, the Chancellor was able to move toward an open acceptance of the Oder-Neisse border without leaving any opening on his right. Following the dramatic victory of the East CDU in the GDR elections on March 18, Kohl was at last able to free himself of the issue.

On June 21 the parliaments of both German states passed with large majorities resolutions recognizing Poland's western border as final and calling for a treaty between Poland and a united Germany after unification. Kohl, in a policy statement to the Bundestag, called the border resolution to be "right and necessary" adding, "Let no one be mistaken: today we face an absolutely clear choice. Either we confirm the existing border or we gamble away the chance for German unity." At the same time he spoke of the 700 years of German history and culture in the areas east of the Oder-Neisse and about the "grave injustice" committed against Germans expelled from the regions.[153] This declaration was deemed insufficient by the Polish government, and Secretary Baker stated in July that the Four Powers might not dissolve their rights and responsibilities in Germany if the two German nations did not provide adequate assurances to Warsaw. This was done in Paris on July 17 following the successful conclusion of the Soviet-German negotiations when a Polish-German agreement was reached at the 2 + 4 talks in Paris.

At the Paris talks the Foreign Ministers of the two Germanies and Poland agreed to five principles concerning the border, including an agreement by a united German government to remove from laws all language referring to the Polish-German border as being provisional; a pledge that the new German parliament would ratify a treaty with Poland confirming the Oder-Neisse line "in the shortest possible time" after unification; an agreement that a united Germany would foreswear any territorial claims and acknowledgement by the Four Powers that they would serve as witnesses that these commitments would be fulfilled.[154]

In November one of the first acts of foreign policy after unification was Kohl's meeting with the Polish Prime Minister at the Polish-German border during which they agreed to sign a border treaty and a broader treaty of economic and cultural cooperation. These were signed in Bonn on June 17, 1991, by Kohl and the new Polish Prime Minister, Jan Krzysztof Bielecki. The treaty committed Germany to help Poland gain membership in the EEC and to assisting Poland to resolve problems created by its foreign-debt burden. While explicitly recognizing the Polish-German border as final, the treaty also contained a promise by Poland to guarantee the rights of approximately 500,000 ethnic Germans living in Poland to speak their language and maintain their traditions. The leaders also signed a mutual non-aggression pact and established youth exchanges and joint environmental and border commissions. Prime Minister Bielecki stated at the signing, "We need the closest possible cooperation with united Germany. United Germany, our especially close neighbor, is Poland's most important partner in all areas."[155]

Although the issue was thus laid to rest, it served as a disquieting portent of how things could go badly in the future of a unified Germany. Kohl's behavior on Poland was in marked contrast to his dealings with Germany's other neighbors and revealed the beginning of a new style in foreign policy which was less encumbered by the weight of the past and more inclined to demonstrate and use the weight of German power. If Germany was becoming a "normal nation," it would act more like France and less like the postwar Federal Republic. In addition, the Chancellor's approach and the suspicion of the Polish government reflected a deep mutual distrust and dislike among the publics of both nations.[156] Finally, his tactics exaggerated the importance of the border issue within Germany itself, as none of the mainstream parties nor much of the public was interested in revising the Oder-Neisse line. He may have pacified or at least neutralized the refugees and expellees and others on the right for the remainder of the year of unification, but the longer-term role of these groups remained uncertain.

THE EAST GERMAN ELECTION

The 2 + 4 process became 1 + 4 sometime during the evening of March 18. As the results from the GDR's first free election became known, it was clear that the forces for rapid unification associated with the Christian Democrats had won a decisive and surprising victory. The CDU and its allies won about half of the vote and were thus in command of the government.[157] Once the new Prime Minister, Lothar de Maizière, formed a grand coalition which included the SPD, the new government had the necessary two-thirds parliamentary majority to push through the constitutional changes needed to rapidly accede to the FRG.

In the days preceding the vote a debate had broken out in West Germany over the right path to unification. The SPD, and to some extent the FDP, argued for the route of a new, all-German constitution as provided for in Article 146 of the West German Basic Law. The Christian Democrats, in contrast, supported entry under Article 23, which provided for German states

(*Länder*) to enter the federation simply by declaration. The Soviets told the West Germans that they were opposed to entry via Article 23 because they feared this would free the new Germany from fulfilling the obligations of the former GDR to the Soviet Union, a position rejected by the Federal Republic.[158]

The March election results made it clear that Article 23 would be the route and that unification would occur sooner rather than later. The choice placed before the East Germans by the election—a reformed GDR or a united Germany—had been decisively answered. The result of March 18 was, as Genscher put it, "a vote for German unification."[159] This put pressure on the parties of the 2 + 4 talks to reach an external agreement for unification before the internal solution made it appear ex post facto.

Chancellor Kohl had seen the Modrow government replaced overnight with the more compliant one of Lothar de Maizière. Although the SPD wished to slow the process of reunification, fearing both the costs and the implications for European stability, they knew that to be seen as blocking or slowing it would mean political extinction in the GDR. De Maizière and his fellow Christian Democrats were political novices with no sense of how to organize or run a government and with little political self-confidence. They were quickly overwhelmed by their rich and experienced West German party leaders. Unification was now to be "Made in West Germany," and the two German governments quickly agreed to an economic and monetary union to take effect on July 1. Germany was, in effect, already unified.

6

Fitting Germany into a New Europe: Establishing the Preconditions for Agreement

SECURITY AND A UNIFIED GERMANY

By early May the major diplomatic issue remaining to be solved was the biggest one: how to fit the new Germany into a future European security arrangement. American support for unification had rested on the assurances of both the Chancellor and the Foreign Minister that they would not sacrifice NATO membership for unity.

The February Camp David meetings produced a reaffirmation by the two governments of their commitment to German membership in NATO along with their agreement that the territory of the GDR should have a "special military status" that took the security interests of all other European countries into account. George Bush and Helmut Kohl agreed that American troops should remain stationed in Germany as a "continued guarantor of stability" and rejected any notion of a Germany belonging to both military blocs.

From Camp David onward the Americans were confident about the German government's commitment to NATO. The British were also reassured and began to play a more important role in shaping the framework for the final agreement. The Genscher Plan was the basis of the Western consensus. The problem was convincing the Soviets that this was also in their best interest.

Although Mikhail Gorbachev had accepted German unification in his Moscow meeting with Kohl and Hans-Dietrich Genscher in February, the Soviet position on NATO membership fluctuated wildly between May and the final resolution in July. While it is difficult to give a definitive answer on what was driving these oscillations, the key factors were most probably

Gorbachev's uncertain domestic power base and the strength of internal resistance to German unification.

While the German issue was one of the most momentous of the era, the Soviet leader was preoccupied with his own mounting domestic problems, especially the growing economic crisis and the challenge to Soviet authority in a number of the republics of the USSR. Gorbachev and his Foreign Minister were reluctant to give their domestic opponents, especially those in the military, the KGB and the party, any pretext for challenging them for having "lost Germany." Foreign policy, which had been, in Genscher's phrase, "the chocolate side of *perestroika*," had come under attack since the opening of the Wall by conservatives.

The Communist Party Congress scheduled for July was a major factor in their strategy, and Gorbachev wished to postpone any final agreement on Germany until he had survived that internal test. The strength of these domestic opponents became more apparent in December 1990 when Eduard Shevardnadze resigned his post in protest against what he warned of as a slide toward dictatorship. In his resignation speech he cited the continuous attacks on him for having sold out the interests of the nation. In 1991 the former Foreign Minister told a Western correspondent that Gorbachev's failure to defend him from attacks by the military for his role in agreeing to German unification was a key reason for his resignation.[160]

Although they were facing strong domestic resistance, the Soviet leaders were being pushed by the pace of internal unification in Germany to reach an agreement while they still had some leverage. As Horst Teltschik described the situation in May following the first 2 + 4 meeting in Bonn, the Soviet Union knows

> that the economic and political stabilization of the GDR can no longer be guaranteed by it [the Soviet Union] itself or any GDR leadership. The stabilization of the GDR can only be guaranteed by the Federal Republic of Germany. . . [After July 1] the process toward German unity will be running at full speed and nobody will be able to stop it unless he wants to create chaos in the GDR.[161]

Furthermore, the economic assistance of the new Germany was seen as crucial by Gorbachev to his modernization of the Soviet Union. To wait too long risked being faced with a fait accompli without the substantial economic rewards that would accrue from settling early with a German leadership eager to wrap up a deal by November.

The only real leverage left to the Soviets was the presence of 380,000 of its troops in the GDR and the implicit potential they represented for delay.

However, this was also a rapidly diminishing asset. It was clear by May that Soviet forces would be out of Czechoslovakia and Hungary by the end of 1991. The Soviet forces in Germany would thus be isolated and strategically exposed, not to mention vulnerable to the enticements of the democracy and a free market economy that would be surrounding them. The rapid deterioration of the morale of Soviet troops that worsened later in 1990 was evidence of this vulnerability.

When Gorbachev allowed the reform process to accelerate in East Germany in the fall of 1989, he probably expected either a reform communist regime under the leadership of a person like Hans Modrow or even a noncommunist regime to stabilize the GDR without hindering closer Soviet-West German relations.[162] If the West Germans were surprised by the fragility of the GDR, why should Gorbachev have been any more prescient? In any case, by the time of his February meeting with Kohl and Genscher, Gorbachev seemed to have accepted that his broad strategy toward Central Europe could not stop short of the unification of Germany but also that this could only be accepted after he had prepared his party and the military for it and had extracted the highest possible price from the thankful West Germans. He consistently thought that he had more time to deal with unification than did Shevardnadze, who in contrast, felt the pressure of events in the GDR.

Kohl and the West German government had, by February 1990, decided that unification must be accomplished by the end of the year. Kohl and Genscher both believed that they had to move while Gorbachev was still in power, or as Kohl put it, "Get the hay in the barn while you can."[163] By mid-January it had become apparent to both Kohl and Genscher that the East German economy was in a dire situation and that Honecker was right when he had declared that mixing capitalism and socialism was like mixing fire and ice. If it was to be done, it had to be done quickly; like a bicycle rider one had to keep moving or fall over. During this same period both Shevardnadze and Baker came to essentially this same conclusion.

In coming to closure on the security arrangements for a new Germany, intense Soviet-German personal diplomacy, supplemented by the good offices of the Americans, was required. Kohl's National Security Advisor, Horst Teltschik, met with Gorbachev six times in 1990, and Genscher spent over sixty hours with Shevardnadze, including two meetings in June alone. These meetings were described by one participant as being "like a seminar on the future order of Europe."[164] The Germans, however, kept the content of these talks largely to themselves. As one American diplomat reported, "We are getting more detailed reports from the Soviets on their meetings than we are getting from the Germans."[165] As the negotiations progressed

Kohl took a larger role, eventually relegating Genscher to a secondary position. One of the main German participants related after unification that the gist of the German conversations with the Soviets was, "What can we do to help you help us? The Soviets told us that the big obstacle is NATO. Can you 'dedemonize' NATO? It would make German unification less difficult for us if NATO appeared in a different position."[166]

The chronology of the Soviet-German deal begins with the Bonn 2 + 4 talks (May 5) and runs through Teltschik's secret meeting with Gorbachev (May 14), the Washington summit (May 31-June 3), the NATO London summit (July 5), the Houston economic summit (July 9-12) and finally the Kohl-Gorbachev agreement in the Caucasus (July 15-16), ratified at the Paris 2 + 4 meeting (July 17), and the final 2 + 4 meeting in Moscow (September).

THE BONN 2 + 4 MEETING

The final push toward settlement began in Bonn on May 5 during the first of the 2 + 4 ministerial meetings. Baker took a conciliatory line in his presentation, emphasizing the need to avoid any singularization of Germany as well as the importance of avoiding the mistakes of the Versailles agreement after World War I. He told the Soviets that they needed the Germans and should reach a settlement which allowed for a strong future Soviet-German relationship. The Secretary of State emphasized the Western conception of 2 + 4 as a process limited solely to the goal of finding a formula for ending Four Power rights in Germany and fully restoring German sovereignty. In regard to security questions, Baker described the 2 + 4 process as a steering group that would decide which European fora would deal with which aspects of German unification, but made it clear that these issues were beyond the mandate of the six.

Shevardnadze came to the meeting with a position approved by Gorbachev and the political leadership that was designed to broaden the 2 + 4 discussions to include security issues. Throughout his statement at the Bonn meeting he stressed the domestic opposition in the Soviet Union to German unification, saying at the opening that "the German angle has loomed extremely large in the Soviet people's national memory, in its perception of the surrounding world and its ideas about the challenges of the times, and in its psychology."[167] While the Soviets no longer feared Germany and now saw it as a partner, "in tackling the external aspects of the unification of Germany, we cannot abstract ourselves from the domestic circumstances in our own country. We are dealing here with an issue of particular importance to the Soviet people and for our entire society." He went on to add again that "neither the current or any other Soviet leadership will be able to neglect public opinion."[168] This statement was not only a signal to the West about the importance of domestic opposition in the USSR but also a reflection of Shevardnadze's own concern that he would have great difficulty selling the unification of Germany to the Soviet public.

The Soviet Foreign Minister, in contrast to Baker's restrictive conception of the talks, offered what he called a "package approach," which would result in a peace treaty that would deal not only with the provisions of Germany's borders, "but should also include provisions on its armed forces, the political military status of the new state, continuity of obligations, a transitional period and measures for this period, and the presence of military contingents of the allied powers on German territory."[169] Specifically, Shevardnadze advocated that Poland must be included in discussions on the border question and that the new Germany must continue to renounce the possession of nuclear, chemical and other weapons of mass destruction.

Shevardnadze restated the opposition of his government to NATO membership for a united Germany, emphasizing, however, that "NATO remains the same as ever—an opposing military bloc with a doctrine which has a definite thrust and which takes the line that it could be the first to deliver a nuclear strike." While the Foreign Minister made a strong case for replacing the military blocs with a new pan-European security system, he left open the possibility of German membership in a transformed NATO.

Shevardnadze then proposed "decoupling" the internal and external aspects of unification, allowing internal unification to occur but postponing the external settlement for a transitional period during which a new pan-European security system could develop. During this period the Four Powers would continue to have a say on German affairs.[170]

Genscher and the chair of the Free Democratic Party, Graf Otto von Lambsdorff's, initial reactions appeared to be open to this possibility. As a source in the Foreign Office explained, Genscher wanted to keep the door open, thereby encouraging Soviet flexibility. Some of Genscher's aides were telling reporters that the proposal would allow the Germans to have their elections and that this was the most important thing. Kohl hesitated at first and considered going along with Genscher but then decided that it was not a good idea as it would singularize Germany. The Chancellor stated the day after Shevardnadze made his proposal that it did not "in any way correspond to my ideas." If accepted the Soviet proposal would have entailed a continued presence of Soviet forces in eastern Germany and thus would have provided them with continued leverage over the Germans. Genscher quickly retreated to Kohl's view.

In addition, the three Western allies held firm and gave the Soviets no encouragement. This was one of the crucial, if brief, moments when things could have gone wrong during 2 + 4. Had the Germans accepted this offer, the diplomatic outcome of the unification process would have been in doubt and the security architecture far less stable than that which did emerge.

At this meeting the Soviet Foreign Minister also agreed that Article 23, which provided for direct accession of the eastern states into the Federal Republic, was an acceptable means for unification. Teltschik summarized the significance of the results of the first of the 2 + 4 meetings as "having shown that no difficulties from the four powers were to be expected on the internal aspects of German unity."[171] The Ministers agreed to future meetings in Berlin, Paris and Moscow and to discuss the question of Poland's western borders with Polish participation and military-political problems with the goal of creating a pan-European security system and the Berlin issue.

On May 14, Teltschik flew to Moscow to hold secret talks with the Soviet leaders. The nature of the visit was so confidential that Teltschik did not even give the air force pilot his name or those of his two companions, officials of the Dresdener Bank, for the passenger list. The talks centered on the Soviet economic crisis. Prime Minister Nikolai Rychkov outlined the severity of the economic situation and the demands by some to return to the pre-1985 system. He asked for financial credits of 1.5 billion Deutsche Marks and a long term credit of DM 10 to 15 billion. Teltschik responded that Kohl assured the Soviet leaders that united Germany would accept all of the GDR's export obligations to the Soviet Union. He indicated as well the willingness of the German government to share the costs of the Soviet troops stationed in the GDR,[172] making it clear to the Soviet leader that this was part of the package to settle all the questions on German unity. He also reminded Gorbachev that it was his turn to invite the Chancellor for a visit, believing that it was important to have the next meeting in Gorbachev's own country as he would be more likely to settle there than to resist further. Although Gorbachev did not agree to a meeting during these conversations, the invitation came soon and Teltschik's thinking proved to be correct.[173]

During these talks, the Soviet President repeated many of the themes laid out by Shevardnadze in his presentation at the Bonn 2 + 4 meeting. He stressed that the best solution would be one that overcame the blocs. It became clear in the discussion that a long-term agreement for Soviet-German economic and political cooperation would be crucial to satisfying the Soviet leaders and would have more importance than a 2 + 4 treaty.

THE WASHINGTON SUMMIT

As the date of the Washington summit approached at the end of May, the West Germans let the Americans know that they expected the Bush-Gorbachev meeting to produce movement on conventional arms control in the Vienna negotiations as well as American offers of economic cooperation and support to the Soviets. In Bonn's view, the Soviet leader had to leave Washington with a success to present to his doubting opponents at home. In addition, Washington had to offer a fundamental change in the relationship between the alliances in order for Gorbachev to swallow the pill of German membership in NATO.[174]

When Kohl visited Bush in Washington on May 17 he reported on Teltschik's recent visit to Moscow and on the growing desperation of the Soviet leader. He told the President that he intended to offer a DM 5 billion credit to the Soviet Union and urged the President to do what he could to support Gorbachev on the basis that it was essential to the West that his reform policies succeed. Bush stated that American domestic opposition to Soviet policies in Lithuania made any support difficult, to which Kohl countered that the Baltics could not determine Western policy.

On the issue of NATO and the U.S. troop presence, the Chancellor made a strong statement of support for the need both for NATO and for a significant American troop presence in Europe. The CSCE could not replace NATO. NATO was essential not only for the protection of the smaller states but also because a Soviet and American withdrawal would leave Soviet forces 600 kilometers from Germany while U.S. troops would be 6,000 kilometers away. Kohl said that a withdrawal of the United States from Europe would be the greatest mistake of the postwar era and assured the President that Germany's leaving NATO would not be the price for German unity.[175] While the President agreed, he said that he did not know how far growing pressures for isolationism would go in the United States.

Kohl told Bush that he believed the Soviets were trying, through public diplomacy, to "dedemonize" NATO, pointing to Shevardnadze's trip to NATO headquarters in Brussels and the invitation for NATO Secretary General Manfred Wörner to visit Moscow. Kohl also made the point that the Helsinki Final Act insured the right of all nations to decide if they wished to belong to an alliance.

Gorbachev came to Washington at the end of May in a weakened position. The Soviet economy was collapsing at an alarming rate and Gorbachev's rival, Boris Yeltsin, was elected President of the Russian Republic on the day before the Soviet President arrived in Washington. German unification was only one of a series of issues to be discussed by Gorbachev and Bush, but it was the one that was the most pressing.

At the Washington summit the Bush Administration presented Gorbachev with the "Nine Assurances" on the future of Germany in the hope of convincing the Soviets that the West was serious about addressing their concerns on NATO membership for Germany. The nine points were a reformulation of the Genscher Plan and other proposals that had been worked out with Bonn and Moscow. Presented as a package, on the suggestion of Robert Zoellick, the main elements were:

- a reaffirmation that a united Germany would remain non-nuclear;
- agreements to limit the size of the Bundeswehr;
- assurances of NATO's willingness to negotiate on short range nuclear weapons;
- a promise to revamp NATO strategy to be less threatening to the Soviets;
- a renunciation of German claims to Polish and Soviet territory;
- a pledge not to station NATO troops in the former GDR;
- agreement for a transitional period for Soviet troops to remain in eastern Germany at German expense;
- a proposal to institutionalize the CSCE to make it a pan-European organization in which the Soviets would play a leading role;
- extensive German economic assistance to the Soviet Union.[176]

The Nine Assurances were the carrots offered in the German-American strategy. If the carrots were not enough, a very large stick remained—the growing momentum of German unification. As a senior American official put it to the Russians during the summit, "We basically said that if you want to engage on these nine points fine. Otherwise you are going to be isolating yourself and antagonizing the Germans."[177]

Gorbachev, however, was not ready to agree. After listening to Bush present what the Soviet leader described as a "rather rigid position" that "a united Germany belong to NATO," he countered with what American officials characterized as "an extremely peculiar" performance with regard to Germany. In an animated way, Gorbachev gave "an extraordinarily vague presentation—it was elaborate, convoluted and imprecise," in which he said that the Soviet people could not accept that the enemy of World War II could now be joined with the enemy of the Cold War (NATO) in one alliance. Germany should be in both alliances until a pan-European security framework could replace the alliances. He closed, however, by asking whether it "shouldn't be the German people who decide whether or not they are in

NATO."[178] President Bush tried unsuccessfully to follow up on this last point.

Gorbachev's senior military advisor, Marshall Sergei Akhromeyev, reinforced the resistance to a NATO solution in an interview during the summit in which he stated that Moscow "could not abide" the integration of German military forces in NATO. He went on to suggest that one option might be the elimination of the military component of NATO's command structure and German membership in a Western alliance structured to consider "purely" political issues. An alternative solution would be a new unified European military alliance with only five members: the United States, the Soviet Union, France, Britain and Germany.[179]

At the close of the summit it was made clear by both sides that there was no apparent movement on the German issues. The Americans believed that Gorbachev would wait until after the July Party Congress before taking a decisive step. It seemed improbable, furthermore, that a Soviet leader would give up the GDR in Washington. So great a concession would have to be made on Soviet soil, with less ostensible pressure.

However, an important sign was picked up from the discussions by American officials. When the Americans told Gorbachev that accepting the Helsinki Declaration meant conceding the right of all European states to join alliances, Gorbachev agreed. Bush communicated this significant response to the Western allies, telling them that he would not make much of this publicly in the hope of avoiding forcing the Soviet leader's hand prematurely.

While there was no public movement on German unification, the summit did produce significant progress on such related issues as the Vienna conventional force negotiations and the institutionalization of CSCE. Prior to the Washington meeting the Soviets had been dragging their feet in Vienna with the obvious intention of emphasizing their opposition to a unified Germany's membership in NATO. In Washington, however, Gorbachev and Bush agreed to reach an agreement by the end of the year, an accomplishment Kohl hailed as "the key to the solution" of a united Germany's status in a new Europe. It also removed the German fear of singularization of their forces for special limits by endorsing a European-wide framework for conventional force reductions.

In a public statement, Kohl once more emphasized Gorbachev's acceptance of the right of the Germans to decide their future. Genscher noted the progress on the institutionalization of CSCE and felt that Baker's promise to move forward (made in a letter on April 24) had been realized.[180] Both German leaders took heart from the qualitative improvement in the nature of U.S.-Soviet relations, remarked upon by both Bush and Gorbachev. Kohl met with Bush at Camp David the weekend after the summit and returned to Germany even more convinced that unification would be completed within the year. He stressed the importance of providing a further reassurance to Gorbachev that German membership in NATO would not harm Soviet interests at the London NATO summit in July.

THE BERLIN 2 + 4 MEETING

The scene shifted from Washington to Berlin, where the second round of the formal 2 + 4 talks was held on June 22. In Berlin Shevardnadze made one last attempt to keep a united Germany out of NATO. On the forty-ninth anniversary of the German attack on the Soviet Union, the Soviet Foreign Minister proposed a transition period of five years, during which Germany would adhere to the international commitments of the two German states. Each part would remain in their respective alliances and the armed forces would be reduced to between 200,000 and 250,000 men. All Allied units would leave Berlin within six months.

While taking this public position, Shevardnadze, however, privately informed the Americans that this was not his plan but one forced upon him and Gorbachev by hard-liners. He had to demonstrate to them that it would not work by presenting it and having it rejected. He openly alluded to this in a press conference when he said that his proposal was not the "final truth" and that he was prepared to look for compromise solutions. The East German Foreign Minister, Markus Meckel, supported the Soviet position, much to the consternation of Genscher, whom he did not bother to consult.

Both Baker and British Foreign Secretary Douglas Hurd forcefully rejected this latest Soviet proposal and held firm to the position that unity must mean full sovereignty, stating that at the end of the 2 + 4 negotiations must come a declaration of the dissolution of Allied rights. Western withdrawal from Berlin could only occur after the Soviets had withdrawn from Germany, although the legal basis of their presence would be changed to a bilateral one rather than one resting on occupation rights.[181] Western solidarity made the Soviets realize the futility of probing any longer for major splits among the Allies. The endgame of German unity was about to begin.

THE NATO LONDON SUMMIT

The NATO summit was held in London on July 5. It had been preceded by a North Atlantic Council meeting in Turnberry, Scotland in early June that had issued the "Message from Turnberry," a declaration that anticipated many of the themes of the London Declaration. Both Turnberry and London provided further proof of the changing balance of power within Europe. As one reporter observed from London:

> Behind the bargaining at the NATO summit this week lies a major power shift that has taken place in the 16 nation alliance over the past year. West Germany is up and calling many of the shots, Britain and France are down and grumbling, and the United States is in the middle, trying to keep everyone happy.[182]

The summit itself was a struggle by Britain and France to hold on to what they could of the status and influence they had in the old Europe while adjusting, however reluctantly, to the emergence of a new Germany and the decline of the Soviet Union. The British and the French were also determined to keep as many of the elements of a strategy that had provided peace in Europe for over 40 years as possible. The Germans were determined to reshape NATO so that it would be seen by the Soviets more as a means for cooperative security than for confrontation. As Genscher had put it in April, "We want to convince the Soviets that the united Germany in the Western Alliance is a contribution to European stability and thereby also an advantage to the Soviet Union."[183] NATO membership, he argued, would be seen as such an advantage only in "a fundamentally changed Europe, in which our alliance not only changes, but in which it is increasingly a factor within new cooperative structures of security and is able to promote disarmament."[184]

Nuclear strategy was the symbolic issue over which the struggle was played out. For the two European nuclear states, France and Britain, the possession of an independent nuclear force had been a vital symbol of national sovereignty and the pillar of their postwar security policies. The leadership in both of these former Great Powers, with far-ranging empires, had resisted being completely dependent upon, and thus subordinate to, the United States. Having been at the center of world affairs for centuries, they were unwilling to accept a second-class status. An independent deterrent muffled the psychological blow of dependency and left London and Paris with at least the myth of control. Nuclear weapons also allowed them to maintain the appurtenance of status within the increasingly limited economic means at their disposal, maintaining status on the cheap.[185]

Nuclear weapons were seen as the prerequisite to Great Power status in the nuclear age.[186] They were viewed as important, therefore, not only in their relationships with the United States but also in relations with other nations. The French, ever concerned about the Germans, saw nuclear weapons as a balance to the political-economic weight of non-nuclear Germany. But British leaders

> were also aware that if Britain abandoned the strategic deterrent her influence within NATO would be reduced. Relative economic decline had only served to highlight the extent to which Britain's influence depended upon her military power, and, more especially, upon the strategic deterrent.[187]

The French and British were also concerned about the ultimate reliability of the American commitment to European security. The experience of both world wars had been that the Americans entered very late and picked up the fruits of victory while minimizing the costs to themselves. And the long, isolationist tradition of American foreign policy was ever-present in the minds of British and French policymakers. The presence both of American troops and of nuclear weapons in Europe was visible evidence of the continuing American commitment to Europe, although the French were convinced that the United States would not remain a European power over the long term.

Although Germany was a non-nuclear state, its political and military leadership had, for a number of reasons, considered nuclear deterrence essential. First, like their French and British counterparts, the German political-military leadership had little faith in the efficacy of conventional deterrence, believing that it had failed regularly in the past while nuclear deterrence had been successful.[188] It was the unique destructiveness of nuclear weapons that made them central to the postwar West German strategic culture.

Second, nuclear weapons have been seen as the most effective and cost-efficient counterweight to Warsaw Pact conventional superiority in Central Europe. Following the failure of NATO to reach the conventional force goals it set for itself in Lisbon in 1952 of 50 allied divisions and 4,000 aircraft (as well as substantial additional future goals), it has been clear that the political will to match Soviet conventional forces was simply not there. European leaders consistently believed that raising conventional forces to the level needed to insure a successful defense of Europe would place politically unacceptable strains on the economies of Western Europe and would raise the specter of a dominant German army as well. Reliance on nuclear deterrence was less costly than the building and maintenance of a robust conventional force and thus has allowed the economies of Western Europe to boom, financing the welfare state and the social consensus it produced.

Third, even if a conventional balance were possible, West German leaders believed that it would be less preferable than reliance on nuclear deterrence. Not only did they lack faith in the deterrent value of conventional forces, but given the geographic compactness of the Federal Republic and its high population and industrial densities, German leaders have believed a conventional war would be as destructive to both Germanies as a nuclear conflict.

The doctrine of flexible response adopted by NATO in 1967 was a compromise between a European demand that alliance strategy threaten early first use of nuclear weapons and an American desire to avoid rapid escalation. Although the doctrine allowed for a pause between conventional and nuclear war, it maintained the centrality of nuclear deterrence.

The end of the Cold War brought many of these interests and assumptions into question in Germany but less so in Britain and France. The Americans were caught in the middle between the pro-nuclear French and British and the new Germany, which was already beginning to doubt the utility of nuclear deterrence in the new Europe. Believing that NATO doctrine had to reflect the diminishing conventional superiority of the Warsaw Pact while at the same time reassure Gorbachev, German leaders and Western publics of the changing nature of the Alliance, President Bush sent a letter to the NATO leaders just prior to the summit proposing a modification in NATO nuclear doctrine away from early first use of nuclear weapons to a strategy of nuclear use as a "last resort."

While the substantive importance of this shift was debatable, with skeptics labeling it merely cosmetic, to the British and the French it signaled a real change away from flexible response in the direction of an operational doctrine of no first use of nuclear weapons. Prime Minister Margaret Thatcher voiced her concern that this shift would make flexible response less flexible and impair the credibility of nuclear deterrence. French concerns were less vocal but just as deep as those of Thatcher. Not being a member of the integrated military command meant that the French could not fully participate in the nuclear debate, but François Mitterrand's views on nuclear deterrence were identical with those of the British Prime Minister. Kohl, in contrast, made no mention in London of flexible response or of any continued need for nuclear weapons in Germany, although the Germans fully supported Bush's proposal.[189]

The result of this quadrilateral negotiation was the London Declaration. Its key elements included the transformation of NATO to include pledges to:

- transform the East-West relationship from one of confrontation to one of cooperation;
- transform the character of NATO's conventional defense both through CFE (conventional forces in Europe) reduction and through a new strategy of "reduced forward presence" to replace that of forward defense; this would include reorganizing NATO troops into multinational corps, limiting their offensive capability and setting limits on the number of German forces;
- modify NATO nuclear strategy away from flexible response to a view of nuclear weapons as a last resort; offer to negotiate on SNF (short-range nuclear forces) and to eliminate all nuclear artillery shells from Europe if the Soviets do the same;
- support the strengthening of the CSCE.

The language on nuclear doctrine was ambiguous, reflecting a compromise between the British/French position and that of Germany. The text read:

> Finally with the total withdrawal of Soviet stationed forces and the implementation of a CFE agreement, the Allies concerned can reduce their reliance on nuclear weapons. These will continue to fulfill an essential role in the overall strategy of the Alliance to prevent war by ensuring that there are no circumstances in which nuclear retaliation in response to military action might be discounted. However, in the transformed Europe, they will be able to adopt a new NATO strategy making nuclear forces truly weapons of last resort.[190]

Bush's reference to "last resort" co-existed with Thatcher's inclusion of the sentence on "no circumstances" in which nuclear retaliation might be discounted. This sentence was designed to leave the Soviets in sufficient doubt about eventual nuclear use to insure deterrence.[191] An agreement announced by the Germans to accept unilateral limits on their forces was a surprise and reversed a policy that had resisted just this sort of an arrangement on the grounds that it "singularized" Germany.

Ambiguous or not, the Germans and the Americans came away from London feeling that they had met their part of the bargain with the Soviets. On the plane trip from London to Houston, Bush sent Gorbachev a message telling him, in effect, "we delivered." He explained the key aspects of the NATO declaration and highlighted the importance of the Warsaw Pact liaison missions in Brussels, which would provide a forum for bilateral East-West military to military contacts, which the summit also accepted.

Added to the developments in NATO were those within the European Community. The Strasbourg summit of December 1989 had already provided a European context for German unification in which the role of the CSCE was raised and German unity firmly embedded within the process of European integration. The Dublin summit held at the end of April developed a concrete framework for the inclusion of the GDR into the EC, and the Commission was hard at work during the summer developing a comprehensive package of regulations and exceptions to be ready by mid-September. At the second Dublin summit, held at the end of June, a deadline of January 1, 1993, was set for ratification of an agreement on economic and monetary union as well as political union, further embedding a united Germany within European structures.[192]

Complementing these tracks of German strategy was the economic one. Drawing the link between economic assistance to the Soviet Union and German unity, Teltschik said, "One can not buy a world power." He then added, however, "You help me and I will help you."[193] This was one of the Great Unspokens of the history of German unification. No one wanted to discuss it openly, fearing that if the impression were created that the Germans were buying the GDR, it would undermine Gorbachev's already precarious position. Yet Kohl became the Soviet's advocate within the West during 1990. During the second Dublin summit and the Houston summit of the G-7 nations the following week, the Chancellor strongly advocated a European aid program for the Soviet economy. He did this for more than German unity, however, believing that a stabilized Soviet Union under Gorbachev's leadership was in the general interest of the West.

Kohl's view was met with skepticism both in London and in Washington. Foreign Secretary Hurd responded, "One doesn't help his friends by throwing a great deal of money in a hole."[194] The American government agreed, remembering the waste of German credits to pre-Solidarity Poland. It also wanted to attach the preconditions that the Soviets end their aid to Cuba, ease up on Jewish emigration and relax its restrictive policy in the Baltic states.

With the conclusion of the Houston summit, the preconditions for a deal on Germany were all in place. The stage was set for a final breakthrough.

7

Agreement in the Caucasus

GORBACHEV AND SHEVARDNADZE
OVERCOME THE OPPOSITION

The London Declaration and President George Bush's message were received as the crucial Soviet party congress got underway in Moscow. Mikhail Gorbachev's team gave the Declaration a positive spin. As a close aide to Eduard Shevardnadze put it later, "Baker delivered everything he promised. We played upon the London Declaration, and stressed the new environment to opponents of unification."[195] The Soviet Foreign Minister commented within forty minutes of the publication of the NATO communiqué, "In London it was declared that the West extends its hand to the East. For our part we are ready to extend our hand to them."[196] This reaction was prepared in advance in anticipation of right-wing resistance. As a Soviet official said later, "We knew [Marshall] Akhromeyev would do a hatchet job. We tried to grab the initiative."[197]

Shevardnadze defended an agreement on German unification at the Party Congress against criticism raised by a number of speakers. His speech, delivered on July 3, offered a concise summary of the logic of his and Gorbachev's strategy on German unification. Shevardnadze emphasized the financial and other costs borne by the Soviet Union as a result of four decades of East-West confrontation. He offered an alternative view of Soviet security that stressed cooperative security over confrontation, pan-Europe over blocs and self-determination over Great Power coercion.

On Eastern Europe he asserted that he, Gorbachev and their colleagues "did predict the changes in principle and sensed that they were inevitable. . . . We felt that if there were not serious changes and reforms, tragic events would ensue. But we were unable on the basis of the principles of the new political thinking to interfere in other people's and other states affairs. I think we acted correctly."[198]

Shevardnadze rejected charges from the floor that the collapse of socialism in Eastern Europe was a defeat for Soviet diplomacy by saying:

> That would be the case if our diplomacy had endeavored to prevent the changes in the neighboring countries, if our relations had deteriorated or worsened with them as a result of this. Soviet diplomacy did not and could not aim to counter the elimination in other countries of administrative-edict systems and totalitarian regimes imposed upon them and alien to them. This would have run counter to the logic of our own actions and the principles of the new political thinking. Moreover, even if what is happening in Eastern Europe were at variance with our interests we would rule out any interference in these states' affairs. This is impossible since we acknowledge not just in words but in actual deeds today the equality of nations, the sovereignty of peoples, non-interference in their affairs and the right of freedom of choice. Any other position involves a return to total chauvinism, the imperial great power mentality, and conflicts with those principles that true Communists have always avowed.[199]

Turning specifically to German unification, the Foreign Minister once again acknowledged the depth of concern about this issue within the Soviet Union, acknowledging it to be natural, given the costs paid during World War II. Added to this, many had gotten accustomed to "certain 'German' realities. We saw them as a guarantee of our security. But let us ponder the following: Can a guarantee founded on the artificial unnatural division of a great nation be reliable? How long can this last?"[200] He pointed to the numerous crises over Germany since World War II and argued that security could be better guaranteed through a "definitive international-legal settlement" in Europe that precluded future wars emanating from German soil.

Shevardnadze pointed to the participation of the Soviet Union in shaping the terms of this settlement. "The German question is being settled with our direct participation and cannot be adopted without our country's consent." He singled out the limitation of the Bundeswehr as an important assurance to the Soviet Union.

> The numerical strength of the Bundeswehr will be considerably reduced within the framework of these reductions. The army of the future "Greater Germany" will be smaller than today's FRG Army. What is best for us? To deal with a 500,000 strong FRG Bundeswehr or, say, an army half that size belonging to a united Germany?[201]

Besides this important limitation, the construction of collective security structures on a pan-European scale had already begun and the confrontation of the blocs was being transformed. Finally, a mutually beneficial relationship with united Germany was emerging. The new Soviet Union would not only get a "peace dividend" from the reduction of defense spending, but it would become an indispensable part of an integrated world.

The Foreign Minister would evoke similar themes later in the year when he defended the final agreement on German unification before the Foreign Affairs Committee of the Supreme Soviet. He argued then that

> the division of Germany is not a natural state . . . [Germany was a threat to the Soviet Union only as long as] a split Germany existed, as long as a mass-scale military confrontation persisted in central Europe. I can say quite responsibly that this threat is ceasing to exist . . . The new Germany is emerging in an entirely new system of European political and military coordinates. It would be difficult for us to change our attitude to Germany's membership in NATO, if the West had not expressed readiness for the establishment of new relations between the two military-political alliances.[202]

The reaction to Shevardnadze's speech at the Congress was moderate, although the hard-liner Valentin Falin restated the unacceptability of NATO membership for united Germany. The response surprised Gorbachev, Shevardnadze and his aides, all of whom expected more resistance to German unification. As one of the top aides in the Foreign Ministry at the time later recounted, "We felt the chill of the psychological reaction within the country. We felt we would not get away easily with any kind of agreement. The reaction was milder than we expected in the party and the population. We expected a more heated debate but the population was focused on internal affairs."[203]

In the face of any real resistance at the Party Congress, Gorbachev and his Foreign Minister felt they had a free hand to settle the outstanding security issues that barred a final resolution of German unification. Gorbachev was to tell Helmut Kohl during the decisive visit to Russia in mid-July that the Party Congress reminded him of John Reed's book on the Bolshevik Revolution, *Ten Days That Shook the World*. "We have eleven days behind us that shook the party."[204]

This was exactly what the Germans had hoped. Although they did not get American pledges of economic assistance to the Soviets either in London or at the Houston economic summit, the German leaders felt ready to make the final push for agreement with the Soviets.

BREAKTHROUGH IN MOSCOW

The first indication of a German-Soviet deal came when the Chancellor received an invitation on July 11 from Gorbachev to include a visit to Stavropol (in the foothills of the Caucasus mountains) during his July trip to the Soviet Union. No other Western leader had been offered such an invitation, and the Germans realized immediately that this was to be no ordinary meeting. Horst Teltschik's reaction was ebullient. "It is done! Gorbachev had invited Kohl to his home. This makes it clear that the visit can not be a failure. We are all agreed that Gorbachev would not have invited Kohl to the Caucasus if he wanted to continue a conflict."[205] On his flight home from the Houston summit, the Chancellor said that the planned trip to the Caucasus would perhaps be "the most important trip of my political career." The Western allies were not informed of the high German hopes for the upcoming meeting because, according to Teltschik, they did not want to raise expectations.

The ground for an agreement had been prepared by the series of summits, the numerous German-Soviet meetings and by Gorbachev's success in defeating his opponents at the Party Congress in early July. The economic groundwork had been laid through a series of agreements by the Germans to increase assistance to the beleaguered Soviet economy, including the five billion DM credit negotiated by Teltschik and extended at the end of June. Kohl was promising a general treaty of economic cooperation as well and had already accepted the need to pay for the stationing and relocation costs of Soviet troops in the GDR. On the security side, Gorbachev had shown new flexibility in mid-June when he spoke of the possibility of West German troops remaining in NATO while those of the GDR would have only associate membership in the Warsaw Pact.[206] Kohl, on his side, had agreed in the London NATO declaration to a limit on the size of the future Bundeswehr.

The method used in Soviet-German negotiations was also important in preparing the final agreement. Genscher and Shevardnadze had reached an understanding during their many discussions to approach issues as blocks of broad problems and to avoid trying to solve the specific issues that each problem complex comprised. As one Soviet participant at the Caucasus meeting described it, " We wanted to go with the minimum of elements— then you will succeed."[207] This approach suited Gorbachev, who wanted an agreement but was not willing to negotiate details.

Kohl flew to Moscow from Bonn accompanied by 134 journalists, including 52 in his plane. Also accompanying the Chancellor on this crucial visit were Genscher, Teltschik, Finance Minister Theo Waigel, Eduard Ackermann, the head of the press section of the Chancellor's Office, Hans Klein, the Chancellor's Press Secretary, Dieter Kastrup, Klaus Blech, the West German Ambassador to the Soviet Union and Juliane Weber, the Chancellor's personal assistant.

Kohl and Gorbachev began with a session that ran over an hour and a half on Sunday, July 15, in Moscow in what proved to be the decisive discussion. Only Teltschik and Gorbachev's advisor, Anatoli Tschernajev, were present (with two interpreters).[208] They met in the Villa Morosov, the guest house of the Foreign Ministry. The German Chancellor opened the meeting with a personal touch, referring to his and Gorbachev's common generational experiences during World War II, both being too young to have been responsible for the war but old enough to have experienced it. Both drew the lesson that their two nations had to overcome their old antagonisms and shape a close and peaceful relationship. Gorbachev reciprocated and emphasized the importance he placed upon a close Soviet-German relationship, a goal equal in importance to the normalization of relations with the United States. The Chancellor declared again his readiness to sign a broad treaty of friendship and cooperation with the Soviet Union, and outlined his recent efforts at the various Western summits to enlist support for Gorbachev's reform policies.

Kohl turned to the situation in East Germany, describing the rapid deterioration of economic conditions in that beleaguered land. He told Gorbachev that he wished he had more time for a transition but the economic decline was too dramatic. It was for this reason that he believed all-German elections on December 2 were so important.

The Chancellor spoke of the three areas that had to be addressed in their talks in order to wrap up the 2 + 4 talks in time for the CSCE conference in November. These points were: an agreement on Soviet troop withdrawals from Germany, the membership of united Germany in NATO and the future ceilings on German armed forces.

The Soviet leader reacted philosophically, quoting Heracles that everything was in flux. Everything today seemed different from when the problems were first discussed, and the time had come to settle the important issues. After further discussion, during which Gorbachev stressed the importance of the changed American policy toward the Soviet Union and his thanks for the German role in this change, he noted that President Bush had been surprised when he told him at the Malta summit that the presence of the United States in Europe contributed to stability. This was the final prologue to agreement.

Gorbachev said a 2 + 4 agreement depended on a united Germany being limited to the two Germanies and Berlin, that Germany would renounce ABC (atomic, biological and chemical) weapons, that the military structure of NATO would not be extended eastward into the former GDR, that the presence of Soviet forces in the former GDR would be regulated under a transitional regime and that the Four Power rights would be dissolved. On the most important question, German membership in NATO, Teltschik recalls Gorbachev's thoughts:

> Gorbachev characterized the membership of united Germany in NATO as the most important question. *De jure* the question is clear, *de facto* this means that the jurisdiction of the NATO treaty will not be extended to the territory of the former GDR. There must be a transitional agreement on rules.

> Quietly and seriously Gorbachev agreed that Germany could remain a member of NATO.[209]

On the heels of this concession Gorbachev offered another. He would not demand a transitional period during which Four Power rights would remain. With the signing of the 2 + 4 agreement, Four Power rights would terminate immediately, although provisions would have to be made for the period during which Soviet forces remained on German soil. After Kohl repeated what he understood had been agreed upon, and Gorbachev confirmed this understanding, it was clear that the final breakthrough had been achieved. Kohl told the Soviet President that the way to Europe for the Soviet Union was through Berlin. He cited a sentence of Bismarck's, that one must grasp the coat of history or be blown away, reportedly to Gorbachev's satisfaction.[210]

As the two leaders emerged from the meeting Kohl turned to his press spokesman, Hans Klein and said, "Everything is settled."[211] At the end of the meeting the two leaders held a press conference during which the Chancellor quoted Gorbachev as saying that we are capable of "cracking hard nuts." To many in the Chancellor's party this was the moment of realization that a deal was done.

AGREEMENT IN THE CAUCASUS

That afternoon the leaders and their entourages flew to the Caucasus and visited a war memorial in Stavropol to the dead of World War II. There, a veteran of that war implored them to do all they could to avoid the rebirth of that old conflict. It is not clear whether this meeting was spontaneous or orchestrated by Gorbachev.

The groups stayed at a dacha in the woods, and it was in this setting that the agreement's details were worked out. The people involved in the meetings were, on the German side: Kohl, Genscher, Kastrup, Waigel and Teltschik and on the Soviet side Gorbachev, Shevardnadze, Finance Minister Valentin Pavlov and Yuli Kvitsinski (the former Soviet ambassador to Bonn and Soviet negotiator at the INF talks) and two aides. The Foreign and Finance Ministers conducted separate talks parallel to the Kohl-Gorbachev discussions.

According to the Germans present, Gorbachev was in a mood to get things done. He was elated that he had carried the day against hard-line opponents at both the Russian Federation Communist Party Congress and the national Communist Party Congress. As one of the Germans who was well informed about what transpired later put it, "The Soviets were willing to concede several points that we didn't expect." The more the Soviets seemed ready to agree the more specific the Germans became in the negotiations. "The Soviets seemed to come with the general idea to say yes. We filled in the details."[212]

The Chancellor and the Soviet leader had spent about 17 hours together on this visit, including time on the plane from Moscow, helicopter rides and private walks. At dinner they talked about topics ranging from Hegel and Kant's concepts of freedom to Gorbachev's anecdotes about Lenin and Brezhnev as well as his complaints about his main opponent, Boris Yeltsin.

After dinner Gorbachev suggested that the two leaders and their Ministers sit together to plan the agenda for the next day's work. Gorbachev, Shevardnadze and Vice Premier for Finance Stepan Sitarjan met with Kohl, Genscher and Waigel. Gorbachev reportedly said, "We need arguments for our people." The discussion centered on security. On the issue of the departure of Soviet troops from Germany, Kohl asked how long this would take, and Gorbachev responded that it would require three to four years. Genscher said that the time limit should not remain open, to which Gorbachev agreed that the process would not last longer than four years. Gorbachev also agreed that since Germany was a sovereign state, NATO-integrated Bundeswehr troops could be stationed in the former GDR after the Soviet withdrawal, but no nuclear weapons could be stationed there. He also agreed that Allied forces could remain in Berlin so long as Soviet forces remained in Germany. Finally the financing of the Soviet troop withdrawal was worked out, with the Germans insisting that this not be viewed as stationing costs but simply as compensation for the effects of the introduction of the Deutsche Mark into the GDR.[213]

By the end of the evening of July 15, agreement had been reached. Kohl did not sleep that night, thinking about the announcement he would make the next day. He stood on the balcony of the dacha, looking at a star-filled sky, thinking, "This is a *Schicksalsnacht* (fateful night) in which a dream was fulfilled."[214]

After a three-hour session on Monday to work out the final details, the two leaders held a joint press conference. Gorbachev allowed Kohl the honor of presenting the details of the agreement.

THE NEW BUNDESWEHR: BACKGROUND TO THE AGREEMENT

To what did the Soviet and German leaders agree? First the Soviets agreed to give up all remaining Soviet claims as a victor power of World War II and occupier of a part of Germany. They renounced as well any restrictions on German sovereignty, maintaining Germany's right to join any alliance of its choice. Kohl made it clear at the joint press conference with Gorbachev that this would be the Atlantic Alliance.

The Germans agreed that the unification of Germany encompassed only the Federal Republic, the German Democratic Republic and Berlin. They agreed to allow the Soviets to withdraw their forces over a three-to-four-year period and to compensate them for the hardships accompanying the introduction of the Deutsche Mark into the former GDR. While all of Germany would be covered by the protection of the NATO treaty, non-NATO German forces from the territorial army would be deployed in eastern Germany until Soviet forces were withdrawn, at which time NATO-integrated units of the Bundeswehr could be deployed in this region. Allied forces would remain stationed in Berlin under bilateral arrangements until all Soviet forces had left German soil, but no foreign troops or nuclear weapons would be stationed in eastern Germany. In short, the Genscher Plan had been accepted, but with some important modifications.

When the plan was initially developed, Genscher had envisioned a demilitarized eastern Germany with a status similar to that of West Berlin in a divided Germany. He held the view that the Soviets would not accept moving NATO east to the Oder-Neisse line and any attempt to do so would jeopardize unification. Therefore no NATO-assigned forces, be they foreign or German, could be deployed in the former GDR. In an internal Foreign Office study written in February, it was argued that this option depended on the readiness of the Soviets to renounce their stationing rights in the GDR and to reduce their presence to a level that was low enough to be acceptable to the German public.[215]

The Defense Ministry strongly opposed this concept, arguing that a demilitarized eastern Germany would create two zones of unequal security and would in effect perpetuate the national division. Yet by the middle of February, specialists in both the Foreign Office and the Defense Ministry had agreed that immediately following the March 18 election, the West German government should issue a joint declaration with the government of the GDR, pledging both governments to a guarantee of the Polish border, a renewed commitment of both Germanies not to launch a war and a renunciation of the possession of chemical, nuclear or biological weapons.[216]

The issue of the stationing of Bundeswehr forces in the GDR came to a head in the middle of February. Defense Minister Gerhard Stoltenberg had taken the position that Bundeswehr units should be stationed in the former GDR. The press reported his position as being that German *and Allied* forces should be deployed in eastern Germany, a position that was immediately attacked by Genscher.[217] A coalition crisis developed over the weekend of February 17-18. Genscher attacked Stoltenberg's position, stating that it would move NATO eastward, arguing that even the stationing of non-NATO German forces would have the same effect. The FDP's defense spokesman in the Bundestag went further, calling Stoltenberg a "political arsonist" and saying that the issue could call into question the continuance of the coalition.[218]

On Monday February 19, a meeting was held between Genscher and Stoltenberg, mediated by Rudolf Seiters, the Chancellor's aide. Seiters was given the charge by Kohl to get an agreement although Seiters had no security policy expertise. Genscher was able to outmaneuver Stoltenberg both in the press and in the face to face meeting, with the result that Seiters got Stoltenberg to back down from the Defense Ministry's position. In a joint statement issued to the press on the 19th, the two ministers reaffirmed the position taken by the Chancellor in a government declaration of February 15 that stated, "no units or installations of the Western alliance should be shifted to the current territory of the GDR." The statement went on to add, "The sentence that no units or installations of the Western alliance should be shifted to the current territory of the GDR *included the NATO assigned and non-NATO assigned armed forces of the Bundeswehr*" [author's italics].[219]

Teltschik, the military leadership and the Ministry of Defense considered this position to be a major defeat. Teltschik held such a declaration to be at least premature in that nothing had been requested along these lines by the Soviets. The Chancellor's National Security Advisor opposed giving away concessions that were not being demanded and getting nothing in return. Internally, the Ministry of Defense held to its original position, hoping to change the government's policy, and the Chancellor's spokesman, Dieter Vogel, stated that this was still only "the beginning of the debate" and that the question "could not be answered today". Genscher had, however, blocked all attempts by the Defense Ministry and the military to participate in the NATO- and defense-related aspects of 2 + 4, arguing that this would give the Soviet military the same right and that Shevardnadze did not want his military involved.

As a result of being cut out of the internal policy process, the German military went to the Americans for assistance and received the backing of Robert Blackwill of the NSC staff and Brent Scowcroft. It was this American support that apparently fortified the Chancellor's resolve to back the Defense Ministry's view and resulted in the West Germans' obtaining Soviet agreement.

Similarly, on the level of limits on the size of the Bundeswehr, the Defense Ministry got close to what it wanted. The German government pledged to limit the Bundeswehr of a unified Germany to a maximum of 370,000 personnel. The Ministry of Defense had wanted to limit German forces to no less than 400,000, while Genscher was willing to go down to 300,000. It is unclear whether Genscher and his deputy, Dieter Kastrup, were taking this position because the Soviets were telling them this was their demand or whether Genscher was pushing this as part of the Free Democrats' domestic agenda. The FDP had been arguing for a reduction in the time of conscript service to nine months, and a figure of 300,000 would have been compatible with this demand. In addition, Genscher had come to view disarmament as "the core of the German question."[220] He feared a hard-line position, be it on the Polish border or on the disposition of the Bundeswehr, could rekindle mistrust of the Germans and thus lose the historic chance for Germany unity. In any case, he and his close aides believed that the fine details of these security issues were not very relevant in the new Europe that was emerging.

On May 24, a decision was to be taken on the issue. Major General Klaus Naumann, at the time the director of the Planning Staff of the Armed Forces (who was to become the Inspector General of the Armed Forces in 1991) and one of the brightest and most influential officers in the Bundeswehr, was in Washington. He learned from the U.S. side that Secretary Baker had raised the Bundeswehr size issue with the Soviets and found that the Soviets had no fixed ideas on numbers. Naumann contacted Teltschik, who informed the Chancellor just prior to his meeting with Genscher and Stoltenberg. Based on this information, Kohl persuaded Genscher to postpone a final decision on the German position on the troop level.

When the issue was raised again within the German government in a series of meetings in July, Kohl spoke of a troop ceiling of under 400,000. Genscher held that any number above 350,000 was too high and would not be acceptable internationally. Stoltenberg held that the position of the coalition, including the FDP, was to keep the length of conscript service to twelve months and that this required a Bundeswehr of at least 350,000 if the draft were to remain equitable. The Defense Ministry position also affirmed that Bundeswehr limits should be placed within the context of conventional force reductions in Europe (CFE) negotiations so as not to singularize Germany, a position supported by the United States as well. Stoltenberg countered with a limit of 370,000 plus a 25,000-man navy (which was kept separate, as naval forces were not included in the CFE negotiations).

The Chancellor retorted that "the final figure should begin with a three" for political reasons. The final compromise was to give the Chancellor a range from 375,000 up to 395,000 with which to work. The figure of 370,000 was reported to the Americans at the Houston summit just preceding the Caucasus meeting. On the plane ride from Moscow to Stavropol, Kohl offered Gorbachev what one of his aides called the "trump card" of a Bundeswehr (including the navy) limit of 370,000.[221] At the final moment, just before the press conference, Gorbachev tried one more time to get Kohl to accept 350,000 as the ceiling. As reported by Hans Klein,

> Kohl had already agreed yesterday in Moscow on 370,000 men. But now Gorbachev said, "Alright [sic], 350,000 men." Kohl was tough. "This I reject. We said 370,000 men. I will not have a *Reichswehr* solution. [Referring to the German army of the 1920s which was limited by the Versailles Treaty.] The reduction of the Bundeswehr and the [East German] National People's Army to a total of 370,000 men is the greatest conventional arms limitation measure that any modern state has undertaken in recent history."[222]

This meant that Kohl split the difference between Genscher's and the Defense Ministry's positions. The Foreign Office also conceded that the limit was part of both CFE and 2 + 4. This meant that even if CFE were not ratified, the Germans would be bound by the manpower limit under 2 + 4. In short, they agreed to the singularization they had tried to avoid—but on their terms.

TELLING THE WORLD

In their joint press conference at the end of the meeting, the leaders praised each other and held out the promise for a deeper relationship in the future. Gorbachev spoke of the importance of the London NATO statement to the settlement on Germany, saying, "If the . . . step of London had not been made, then it would have been difficult to make headway at our meeting." He alluded to the limits of choice left to him in reaching agreement by adding that "we made *Realpolitik*. We have taken as a basis today's reality, the significance for Europe and the world." Gorbachev noted, however, his belief that the Germany with which he was dealing was not the one that had invaded the Soviet Union.

> When we laid down the wreaths at the war memorial and we met the war veterans, they told us that it was necessary that there be a united Europe, and that our relations have to be peaceful, and that what happened should not repeat itself. And these were people who themselves suffered under Hitler's fascism .
> . . I think he [Mr. Kohl] is a responsible politician, and here the good will of the Germans was expressed, and it met with the satisfaction of our people.[223]

He also said that the Germans "have shown in their postwar history that they are for democracy, that their policy is that no war should arise from German soil, that they are open to cooperation with other nations. Without this nothing would have happened."

Kohl was effusive calling the breakthrough a "fantastic result." The talks, he said, "were very candid and marked by understanding and personal sympathy." Kohl stressed the future importance of Soviet-German relations.

> It is clear to me and President Gorbachev that German-Soviet relations have a central significance for the future of our peoples and for the fate of Europe. . . .

> The geopolitical situation of Germany determines that Germany is in a central position. We have been an area through which armies went from west to east. But it has also been a bridge for ideas and culture . . . The development of German and Russian culture is not thinkable without this mutual fertilization.[224]

Kohl spoke of an agreement to conclude an all-encompassing bilateral treaty immediately after unification, to include questions of political relations, security, economics, culture, science and technology, youth exchanges and other matters. German officials made it clear that the offer of a comprehensive treaty assured Gorbachev that the Soviet Union would not be locked out of the new Europe.[225]

The reaction to the agreement was one of surprised approval. Some of the journalists present at the press conference reacted with disbelief to the announcement of the acceptance of German membership in NATO and the confirmation of a limit of 370,000 for the Bundeswehr. The NATO allies expressed approval at the agreement on NATO membership, but some were concerned that this important agreement was struck in a bilateral forum without any advance warning. Many resented that the Soviet-German deal upstaged the wider 2 + 4 and CSCE accords scheduled for later in the year.

The Americans were taken by surprise, as the thinking in Washington had been that a final Soviet agreement would not come at the earliest until September because of Gorbachev's domestic problems. They were told by the West Germans that they, too, were surprised and had not expected such an early agreement. Secretary Baker's reaction produced one of the more memorable quotes of the year, described by one correspondent as a response "with a circumlocution that left even diplomats scratching their heads." When asked if he was surprised after learning of the agreement from news reports, Baker said, "This is a delightful surprise to the extent that it is a surprise, and it is only a surprise to the extent that we anticipated."[226]

Some American officials were disappointed that Kohl did not extend Bush the courtesy of a phone call prior to announcing the agreement to the press. The Chancellor's aides explained the lack of notification as the result of logistics. They were in an isolated area without access to telephones and secure communications. In any case, while the Americans were surprised by the extent of German economic assurances to the Soviets, the overall settlement was in line with what the United States had expected.

Suspicions arose among many in the West of secret agreements and a new Rapallo. French officials, for example, are reported to have concluded, "Kohl negotiated the July 16, 1990 agreement on German membership in NATO directly with Gorbachev, making the 'two plus four' negotiations seem like a *pro forma* framework of secondary importance."[227]

Were promises made concerning future economic assistance and the future of Allied forces and nuclear weapons in united Germany? Although both Kohl and Gorbachev denied any such agreements, the question will remain for years. It is unlikely that such agreements were, in fact, made but, agreements or not, the Soviets assumed that the natural dynamics of public opinion in united Germany would push future German governments in these directions. As one of the Soviet officials involved described it later, "The Soviet Union was not interested in pushing the United States out of Germany. As concerned nuclear weapons, the dynamics of the situation would take care of itself. Nuclear weapons would not sit well with German independence."[228] In any case, the agreement had been worked out with the Western allies, especially the United States, and could not correctly be characterized as having been reached unilaterally by the Germans.

Kohl flew back to Bonn on July 17. During the flight he walked back to the press section and shared a glass of champagne in a toast to the full sovereignty of Germany. A number of correspondents offered the Chancellor congratulations, a unique tribute from a group not known for its enthusiasm for Kohl.

8

The Final Settlement

DETAILS OF THE TREATY

The final meetings of the 2 + 4 talks, in Paris on July 17 and in Moscow on September 12, were anticlimactic. The Paris meeting ratified the agreement on the Polish border. The meeting in Moscow completed the process with the signing of a short Treaty on the Final Settlement with Respect to Germany. (The text of the treaty can be found in the appendix at the end of this volume.) The treaty was not a peace treaty, as peace treaties regulate the legal problems resulting from a war such as termination of the state of war and the reestablishment of diplomatic relations. These had been resolved for some time.[229] Furthermore, a peace treaty would have reopened settled questions, such as reparations, and would have treated the Germans as the vanquished and its allies as the victors. The treaty did not mark the end of World War II but rather the end of the Cold War, just as the division of Germany had been the consequence of the latter rather than the former.

Article 1 of the treaty deals with the border questions. It states clearly that united Germany comprises of the two former German states and Berlin. It commits the new Germany to reach a binding treaty with Poland that recognizes the existing border. United Germany "has no territorial claims whatsoever against other states and shall not assert any in the future." Furthermore, it pledges that the constitution of united Germany "will not contain any provision incompatible with these principles," specifically referring to the preamble, the second sentence of Article 23 and Article 146 of the Basic Law. With this article, Germany finally gave up 114,000 square kilometers—Silesia, East Brandenburg, Pomerania and East Prussia—a quarter of its prewar territory.

Article 2 reaffirms the declarations of the two German states to renounce aggression, a commitment already contained in international law and Article 26 of the Basic Law and reaffirmed as well in the new general treaty with the Soviet Union.

Article 3 reaffirms the renunciation of the manufacture and possession of and control over nuclear, biological and chemical weapons, and specifically commits united Germany to continue to adhere to the Treaty on the Non-Proliferation of Nuclear Weapons of July 1, 1968. The two governments also supported the August 30, 1990, statement of the West German government in Vienna at the CFE negotiations, which pledged a reduction of the Bundeswehr (air, ground and naval forces) to a level of 370,000 over a three-to-four-year period. This, however, is a mere repetition of a statement and is not a renewed commitment. The statement also links the reductions to the successful conclusion of a first CFE agreement, again with the intent of avoiding the singularization of Germany by placing reductions in the Bundeswehr alongside reductions by other European states.

Article 4 commits the Soviet Union to withdrawing its forces from the former GDR by the end of 1994. The conditions for and the duration of the Soviet military presence as well as the conduct of their withdrawal are to be settled by a bilateral agreement. There is a link between this withdrawal and the pledge to limit the Bundeswehr contained in Article 3. This may imply that the Germans are committed to a 370,000 force ceiling under this treaty independent of a CFE agreement and that the Soviets could delay their withdrawal if Germany fails to fulfill its commitment on the size of its forces. It would codify a "singularization" of Germany separate from a multilateral arms control agreement and commit it to these reductions even if CFE is not ratified. However, when the discussions in the Caucasus are reviewed it seems clear that the Germans only agreed to link the 370,000 ceiling to the CFE discussions.[230]

Article 5 regulates the military status of what would become the former GDR. It states that during the transitional period when Soviet forces are being withdrawn from Germany, "only territorial defense units which are not integrated into alliance structures to which German armed forces in the rest of German territory are assigned will be stationed" in the territory of the GDR. This means that no NATO-assigned German forces can exist in the eastern Länder (federal states) until Soviet forces are gone. Allied forces may remain in Berlin upon German request during this transition period on the basis of bilateral agreements, not as occupying forces. Their size cannot exceed that at the time of the signing of the treaty, and new categories of weapons may not be introduced.

Paragraph 3 of this Article states that once Soviet forces are withdrawn from Germany, NATO-assigned German forces may be stationed on the territory of the former GDR, but without nuclear weapons carriers. Dual-capable systems that are equipped for a conventional role in West Germany may be deployed in the eastern Länder. But foreign armed forces and nuclear weapons or their carriers will not be stationed in that part of Germany or deployed there." Under this paragraph, the eastern Länder become a nuclear-free zone.

The last sentence, concerning "deployment" of foreign forces, created a last-minute mini-crisis in the talks. During the negotiations in the Caucasus, Helmut Kohl and Hans-Dietrich Genscher had insisted that the restriction on the deployment of NATO forces into the former GDR held only during the period that Soviet forces remained in Germany. Once the Soviets were out, Germany as a sovereign state had the right to do what it wished on its territory. Mikhail Gorbachev agreed but stated that the common understanding would be that sovereign Germany would take Soviet security interests into consideration when it made decisions in this area and that nuclear weapons would not be stationed in this part of Germany. The German and Soviet leaders also agreed that foreign troops would not be transferred to the territory of the former GDR after Soviet forces were withdrawn.[231]

On the evening before the treaty was to be signed, British Foreign Minister Douglas Hurd informed Genscher that he could not sign the treaty because his government insisted on the right of NATO forces to maneuver in the former GDR after the Soviet withdrawal. This had been a British position for weeks that had caused frictions with the Germans, who knew this was unacceptable to the Soviets. As one German diplomat was quoted as saying, "We sense displeasure that they [the British] no longer have their role."[232]

The Germans, both eastern and western, viewed the agreement to allow a Soviet presence in Germany for four years as already an infringement of sovereignty. As one present put it, "We couldn't allow this to prevent German unity." Lothar de Maizière told the West Germans, "Can you imagine me going back to Berlin and saying we can't have unity because of the British desire for maneuvers?" Genscher was incensed and told Hurd, "We will see who doesn't come tomorrow. The world press will see where the guilty will be sitting."[233]

After a frantic night of discussions, during which Secretary James Baker was awakened by an angry Genscher with a request for mediation, the British finally agreed to a minute to the treaty drafted during the night by Dieter Kastrup, which stated that the German government would decide any questions that arose concerning the meaning of the word deployment in a "reasonable and responsible way taking into account the security interests of each contracting party."[234]

Article 6 affirms the right of united Germany to belong to alliances. Article 7 terminated the rights and responsibilities of the Four Powers relating to Berlin and Germany as a whole and recognized full sovereignty for united Germany over its internal and external affairs. Germany, in short, had the right to join alliances.

THE FINISHING TOUCHES

The treaty did not come into force on October 3, the day the East German Länder joined the Federal Republic, as it required ratification by all the signatory states. The Four Powers agreed in New York on October 1, 1990, to suspend their rights and responsibilities relating to Berlin and Germany from the moment of German unification until the coming into force of the treaty. The idea of suspension was invented by the British embassy in Bonn as a means for ending Four Power rights without a lengthy ratification period and also as a lever to insure that the Poles got a border treaty with united Germany before termination of Four Power rights.

In addition, the Germans and the Soviets initialed on September 13 the Treaty on Good Neighborly Relations, Partnership and Cooperation between the two nations. Last-minute bargaining over the size of the German contribution for the housing and resettlement of Soviet forces resulted in an agreement by the Germans to pay $ 7.5 billion to the Soviets for these costs. Genscher referred to this as "the price of unity."[235] The CSCE conference met in Paris on November 19-21 to give a broad European blessing to unification. On October 3, Germany was a sovereign state. Reunified Germany was, however, not a new state but, legally at least, an extension of the Federal Republic of Germany with five new states or Länder. The legal obligations of the Federal Republic remained as well as the new ones taken on from the former German Democratic Republic.

In a final irony, the final days of the most momentous event of postwar European history occurred almost unnoticed. The Soviets were preoccupied by their mounting domestic problems while the United States and much of Western Europe were focusing their attention on the crisis in the Persian Gulf set off by Iraq's invasion of Kuwait. Yet Eduard Shevardnadze, just prior to his resignation as Foreign Minister at the end of the year best summed up what had been achieved. "The German question, this great and classical problem of world politics that yesterday seemed insolvable, was solved peacefully and with satisfaction on all sides."[236]

9

2 + 4: An Assessment

DOGS THAT DIDN'T BARK:
THINGS THAT COULD HAVE GONE WRONG

The players in the 2 + 4 process achieved what they set out to accomplish—managing an event with great implications for political, economic and military balances in Europe in a way that did not produce any visible losers or major conflict. As Chancellor Helmut Kohl put it, this "was the first unification of a country in modern history achieved without war, pain or strife."[237]

The smoothness of the process and its stunning rapidity, "a world record of diplomacy," as Christoph Bertram described it,[238] may lead the observer to overlook how easily things could have gone wrong. It is important for the historian, as Hugh Trevor-Roper notes, to consider what might have happened. "At any given moment [in history] there are alternatives and to dismiss them . . . because they were not realized is to take the reality out of the situation."[239]

As Chancellor Kohl's statement suggests, great historical shifts in power relationships such as the one that occurred in Central Europe in 1989 and 1990, are often accompanied by great violence, revolution and war. While it is too soon to begin to assess the long-term stability of the settlement of 1990, the transformation will be judged by historians as a remarkably smooth one. Yet this was far from inevitable.

It may not be known for decades how close Central Europe came to war in 1989, but Mikhail Gorbachev's decision not to use force to hold East Germany surely earned him the Nobel Peace Prize he later received. As Eduard Shevardnadze publicly stated after his resignation as Soviet Foreign Minister in December 1990, there were strong voices in the Soviet Party, military and KGB urging the Soviet leader to use force to prevent the loss of East Germany at least twice in 1989, in August and then again in October. Had the Soviet leadership decided to invoke the Brezhnev Doctrine in 1989, the possibilities for escalation would have been much higher than in any of the crises of the Cold War. The Berlin Wall would have been breached, hundreds of thousands of East Germans would have fled West and Allied and Bundeswehr units would have been drawn into a dangerous confrontation with East German and Soviet units.

Both the German and the American governments were nervous in October and November 1989 about the possibility of the Soviet or East German military acting in an attempt to stop the growing revolution in East Germany. This caused the two countries to act with great caution in their initial reactions to the fall of the Wall. They seem to have been satisfied in December by assurances from Gorbachev that he would not use force, but history was kind, not only in granting the Soviet leader the wisdom of his decision, but also in the continuity of Gorbachev and Shevardnadze as leaders of the USSR during this critical year. The discipline of the East German demonstrators was also crucial in containing the explosiveness of the situation.

Another minor miracle was the acquiescence of the feared Stasi to their fate without recourse to the path of bloody resistance taken in Romania by Nicolae Ceausescu's Securitate. Here as well the Soviet decision, as communicated both by the military and the KGB, was vital. Because the GDR was among the most integrated states within the Soviet security system, the Stasi and the Volksarmee had little competence to begin action independent of Soviet policy. Romanian independence from the Soviet Union, in contrast, gave the Securitate more freedom of action.

The Romanian comparison illustrates the qualitative difference of the change in East Germany from that which occurred in the other former Warsaw Pact states in 1989. Bloody revolution was one thing in Romania. It was quite another in East Germany. Romania was isolated, while Germany was the key to the European balance. Thus one of the great "might have beens" was what might have happened if Gorbachev had not done what he did in the GDR or if he had been replaced during the German Revolution with someone like Yegor Ligachev? For all of the luster that Gorbachev lost as a reformer after 1990, he should be remembered for this great act of historical judgement and courage. It is unusual for a Great Power to acquiesce so peacefully to so sudden a reversal of its fortune and so steep a loss of its prestige while maintaining such impressive military capabilities and advantages.

The other "what ifs" are less dramatic but worth considering. What if the United States in November and December had chosen the position taken by France and Britain after the fall of the Wall? Had the American Administration been as reluctant about unification as the two other western Allied powers, Soviet policy could have turned out very differently. At the very least the speed toward unity would have slowed and support for Chancellor Kohl's drive for unification could have been delegitimized at home by the Social Democrats, whose candidate for Chancellor, Oskar Lafontaine, was already voicing opposition to the pace and cost of unification, and abroad.

Many have been critical of the American policy of, as one National Security Council staffer put it, "the faster the better" regarding unification. No matter what the longer-term consequences of a united Germany are, it is fair to conclude that the American policymakers acted wisely given the historical circumstances of the time. A slower approach almost certainly would have alienated the Germans and led to a less favorable settlement as the Germans might well have been tempted to cut a different sort of deal with the Soviets. It might well have revived feelings of victimization on both the right and the left in Germany and boosted the vote of the far right Republikaner, a party whose prospects were dimmed (at least temporarily) when Kohl grasped the mantle of unification. This was a concern voiced in November 1989 by President Richard von Weizsäcker and was not unnoticed by Helmut Kohl.

Rather than with anti-American resentment, the German public came out of unification with strong feelings of approval for the United States and its support for unification. While this gratitude may have a short shelf life in the world of politics, it provided a much sounder basis for the beginning of a new era in German-American relations than the resentment that opposition to unification could have engendered. That the Germans entered the post-Cold War era feeling like winners stands in marked contrast to the feelings of victimization in Germany that characterized the Versailles system.

Another "might have been" deals with the leadership of Kohl and Genscher during this fateful year. They tended to work much better as a team than they did before the year of unification, each compensating for the other's weakness and checking possible excesses that might have gone unchecked without the other in the coalition. Genscher helped to keep the Polish border issue from derailing international support for unification and did much to gain Soviet trust and eventual acceptance of a united Germany, while Kohl, with some assistance from the American government, modified the Genscher Plan in ways that led to a more, rather than less, secure Germany.

Although Genscher in many ways was both a forerunner and a reactor to events, anticipating the shape of things to come and not only reacting to them, he often overestimated what the Soviets would require for a settlement and was willing to concede more than he needed to. He seemed ready to accept the dangerous proposal Shevardnadze made at the May 2 + 4 meeting in Bonn to decouple the internal and external aspects of unification. Kohl's firm rejection averted a potential crisis within the Western delegations.

More importantly, had Genscher's position of February 1990 that no Bundeswehr forces be deployed in the former GDR held, the new Länder would have been placed in a singularly more exposed position than that which emerged from the agreement. Genscher was also willing to settle for a much smaller Bundeswehr than he had to in terms of Soviet demands. In both cases Kohl, with the aid of the Americans, was able to create a more viable German position and final outcome.

The cooperation between Genscher and Kohl was greatly facilitated by the outcome of the March 18 elections in the GDR. Had (as many predicted) the SPD won the elections, the internal dynamic and self-confidence of the CDU-CSU-FDP coalition would have been shaken. The Soviets may well have raised their terms for settlement or even reassessed the need to accept German unification. The election, rather, confirmed for both leaders that their political interests and the historical moment both argued for close collaboration rather than open competition.

A NEW STATECRAFT

Why did so much that could have gone wrong go right? Beyond good fortune, the credit has to go to the few people who made it happen. Although the East German public created the pressure for change, the leaders of the Soviet Union, the United States and West Germany were crucial to the smooth handling and peaceful resolution of this historic sea change. As has been observed throughout this volume, at a pivotal moment of history the right people were at the right place at the right time and did the right thing. Karl Kaiser's felicitous phrase rings true: The diplomacy of German unification was "*ein Glücksfall von Staatskunst*" (a fortunate case of statecraft).

Instead of Kaiser Wilhelm or Hitler, Germany produced the less charismatic but wise statesmanship of Kohl and Genscher. The United States was led by men who, while not visionaries, were pragmatists with a sense of what history offered. In the Soviet Union, Gorbachev was an indecisive political Jekyll and Hyde figure, pulled between his broader vision of a new Europe and a reformed Soviet Union on the one side and his limited reformism and political opportunism on the other. Although he seemed to be more a masterful tactician than a strategist, his sense of what was possible and what was irretrievable was crucial whenever key decisions had to be taken.

If one person must be singled out as the most crucial to the outcome, Eduard Shevardnadze stands out. Gorbachev was ultimately responsible for the decisions taken, and his exercise of restraint was decisive, but it was the Soviet Foreign Minister who was the moving force behind the revolution in the Soviet position on Germany. He was consistently in front of Gorbachev in recognizing the importance and the nature of the changes occurring in Europe and the broader international context. He worked out the details of the grand compromise on Germany and sold them to the Soviet President. Unlike his American and West German counterparts, Shevardnadze was operating in a policy environment in which he faced great opposition and ran a high personal and political risk. He had to engineer a strategic retreat and to structure acceptance of a great defeat in terms of postwar Soviet foreign policy objectives. It was evident at the end of this process that the shift in the Soviet position was the key to German unity and that Shevardnadze was the person most responsible for that shift.

It was a fortunate case of statecraft not only because of the quality of the people involved but also due to the continuity of these people throughout a brief but often frenzied period. Within a few months of the end of the process in October 1990, Shevardnadze was gone as Foreign Minister, Horst Teltschik was out of government and the Gulf War became the riveting preoccupation of the Americans who had shaped 2 + 4. These statesmen shared an understanding of the need to produce only winners, or at least to avoid creating losers. They had an empathetic quality that allowed them to place themselves in the others' shoes, to understand their interests and needs.

The people were important but so was the process. In this age of democratic diplomacy, conducted under the constant scrutiny of ever more pervasive media, 2 + 4 was a case of elite diplomacy carried out by a few political officials with little engagement of the vast bureaucracies or political parties in these large nations. It was diplomacy without many diplomats in the traditional sense of the term. Foreign Service officers, along with large segments of the national security bureaucracies in all three of the key nations, were kept largely on the sidelines. Negotiations were conducted and agreements reached through personal contacts sped by telecommunications and jet travel. Embassies were largely circumvented. The result was agreement on a complex set of issues in record time. All the participants were continually aware of the press of time and need for rapid agreement because they were trying to create a stable structure out of a revolutionary situation, both in Germany and in the Soviet Union.

This model of diplomacy may be the model for the way nations will conduct their relations on vital issues in the future. The technological revolutions of the late twentieth century have made the old roles of diplomats, embassies and bureaucracies both irrelevant and even dysfunctional to political leaders intent on shaping their own agendas. CNN (Cable News Network), faxes, cellular phones and government jets have replaced ambassadors in the key function of communication between nations, at least in certain types of policy areas. This model, however, remains less suitable for the day-to-day management of technical issues that require bureaucratic expertise. It is more effective in dealing with a priority issue in a concentrated and time-sensitive manner, but is liable to miss emerging crises and to neglect non-priority concerns that may soon become high priority items.[240]

In addition, this "New Diplomacy" may not be effective in building a national consensus behind a policy. For example, a key problem for the Soviets emerged in the wake of the Caucasus agreement as a result of the nature of the Soviet decision process. The deal on Germany was struck by the leadership of the Foreign Ministry and had been presented to the Soviet military. This was a break from the traditional pattern of Soviet decision making and opened up questions for the future. The close cooperation between Shevardnadze, Baker and Genscher only increased the military's suspicion of the Foreign Minister and of the deal he had cut. The resistance that emerged in the fall and winter after unification and that culminated in the resignation of Shevardnadze and the long delays in reaching agreement on CFE and in Soviet ratification of the 2 + 4 accords all indicated the cost of pushing through such a significant agreement without a broad consensus within the Soviet government.

This weakness was not apparent in the American case because of the broad public support for German unification. However, as a well-informed observer of the Baker State Department later noted, this closed style of decision making has its political costs.

> When the world all seemed to be coming their [Bush and Baker's] way, with Communism crumbling on their watch, they got by with their elitist "we know best" approach, with decisions being made in a very close circle without either man explaining policies to the American people to summon support or articulating the emotion of a moment for a nation hungry for a voice.

Speaking about the Cold War's end, one White House official said, "People don't feel good about what is happening, because they have never been told why they should."[241]

WINNERS AND LOSERS

The United States

The Americans involved in the process viewed its outcome as highly successful. Their assessment is justified by the record. They achieved their primary objective of keeping a unified Germany within NATO as set out by President Bush in his Four Principles and elaborated by Secretary Baker in his Berlin speech of December 12. In addition, U.S. and allied forces would remain in a unified Germany on a new bilateral basis. The Polish border issue was put to rest and outstanding U.S. citizen claims against the GDR will be settled. The new Germany was very grateful to the Americans for their support, in contrast to the residue of resentment left by the French and British policies.

Although some have argued that the United States had no other option but to jump on the speeding locomotive of German unity while others contend that the Bush Administration did not shape events but followed them, it seems clear that American policy was well thought out and decisive to the outcome.[242] The Bush Administration shaped the 2 + 4 framework and helped to forge the final agreement on the security status of united Germany. It played a central role in the construction of a post-Cold War European security architecture, taking the lead at the NATO London summit in recasting NATO strategy. Its early support of German unification reassured the West German government and insured close Western cooperation. This would not have been the case had the United States been less helpful and followed the path initially taken by the British and French. The Americans also reassured the Soviets throughout the year of unification and played an important role in gaining their acceptance of German unification within NATO.

American policy succeeded because it was well conceived and smoothly coordinated. The Bush Administration recognized earlier than any other government involved the significance of the developments in Germany and where they were heading. It welcomed the trends that it saw emerging and viewed them as being in the long-term interests of the United States. It could rely on a public, political and intellectual climate that was supportive of its efforts and never had to worry about serious domestic opposition to its course of action, as the unanimous vote of 98 to 0 in the Senate for approval of the final treaty demonstrated. The key players in the Administration worked well together, avoiding the rancor and infighting of previous Administrations. Finally, in Chancellor Kohl and Foreign Minister Genscher it had partners who were trusted and who worked closely with the Americans. The events of 1989-1990 demonstrated the importance of a close German-American partnership for dealing with critical changes in Europe.

The Soviet Union

If the objectives of the Soviet Union are evaluated by the outcome of 2 + 4, it would seem that the USSR was less successful than the United States. If the Soviet objective was a neutral Germany, then it clearly failed in its policy. However, this was not the objective of either Gorbachev or Shevardnadze. Gorbachev had already told President Bush at Malta that he wished to have the United States remain in Europe, and it is unlikely that he wished to have a Germany without a solid anchor in the West. Neutrality was the objective of the Imperial Conservatives, people such as Marshall Sergei Akhromeyev, Yegor Ligachev, Valentin Falin and perhaps Yuli Kvitsinski, and they, rather than the reformers, were the losers on this count. It is apparent from the lack of public outrage at the settlement that the Soviet people did not consider the result of united Germany remaining in NATO to be detrimental to their interests, or they at least considered it to be of little relative importance.

If one looks at the limits on the German military that were achieved in 2 + 4, then Gorbachev could claim that he was successful in what was probably a more important objective for the Soviet Union. The German military was limited to a size that was substantially smaller than that of the Russian Republic or possibly even of the Ukraine. It was committed to remaining a non nuclear power as well and could not extend its own or its allies' military reach into Eastern Europe. In addition, NATO was in the process of being transformed after the London Declaration, and it was apparent even in October 1990 that American forces in Germany and in Europe would be substantially reduced over the coming decade.

In the broader context the goal of both Gorbachev and Shevardnadze to end the confrontation of blocs in Europe and to replace it with a more pan European system was closer to achievement as a result of German unification. Although the hopes that they had for the CSCE seemed to go unfulfilled, the evolution of NATO and of the cooperative Soviet-American relationship was what the Soviet leaders had in mind. The confrontation of the blocs ended with the unification of Germany. The final border settlement met the initial Soviet objective. Not only was the Polish-German border recognized as final, but the unification of the FRG, GDR and Berlin also meant than any other possible border claims by Germany were foreclosed.

Finally, the Soviets achieved their primary goal of obtaining a closer German-Soviet relationship and substantial economic and technical assistance for the modernization of the Soviet economy. For the Soviets, the Treaty of Good Neighborly Relations, Partnership and Cooperation initialed during the Moscow meeting, was more important than the 2 + 4 Treaty. United Germany made a commitment of DM 13 billion to cover the cost of subsidizing and relocating Soviet forces and building them housing in the Soviet Union. The treaty's twenty-two articles created a German-Soviet economic partnership that made Germany the most important external support of Gorbachev's economic reforms. The Germans pledged not only to aid the Soviet economy but also to assist its entry into world economic organizations.

Most importantly, German unification was a crucial step toward the actualization of Gorbachev and Shevardnadze's long term strategy of modernization, integration and humanization of the (former) Soviet Union. As Shevardnadze put it to Communist Party members in the Foreign Ministry in the spring of 1990:

> The belief that we are a great country and that we should be respected for this is deeply ingrained in me, as in everyone. But great in what? Territory? Population? Quantity of arms? Or the people's troubles? The individual's lack of rights? Life's disorderliness? In what do we, who have virtually the highest infant mortality rate on our planet, take pride? It is not easy answering the questions: Who are you and who do you wish to be? A country which is feared or a country which is respected? A country of power or a country of kindness?[243]

Shevardnadze and Gorbachev (probably in that order) had a long-term view that guided their approach on Germany. They believed that Soviet policy since Stalin had led to the bankruptcy of the USSR and had resulted in its isolation and exclusion from the Western mainstream. Only after, as Gorbachev's press spokesman Gennadi Gerasimov phrased it, "we take away the threat" was it possible for the Soviet Union to rejoin the mainstream with the hope that it could enter the twenty-first century in the First World rather than in the Third.

The jury will be out on the success of this strategy for a long time, but, even after the breakup of the Soviet Union and the fall of Gorbachev, it was a sound approach that holds out the prospect of a democratic and modern

Russia in a democratic Europe. Shevardnadze was surely right (as he echoed the words of George Kennan, spoken thirty-five years earlier) in believing that, as he said before the Supreme Soviet in defense of the final treaty on Germany,

> the division of Germany was not a natural state . . . Germany was the focus of the Cold War and confrontation. The two major armed groups confronted and are still confronting each other here.

> The situation here has been exacerbated more than once, placing the world on the brink of war. This could not and should not last. Did the Soviet people win the last war to continue living under the permanent danger of having to withstand yet another military threat coming from German soil? One must look the truth in the face: This was a major threat as long as a split Germany existed, as long as a mass-scale military confrontation persisted in central Europe.[244]

Britain and France

Britain and France came out of the process diminished both in power and in status. They tried to play a spoiler's role in the beginning and then had to accept the outcome agreed upon by the Germans, Americans and Soviets. While German unification was bound to shift the intra-European balance away from these two victor powers of World War II, both could have adjusted more gracefully and profitably to this great historical change. They both looked ineffectual in their attempts to prevent what seemed to be increasingly inevitable.

Both, however, soon adjusted to the new relationships shaped by German unification and moved toward more cooperative and sensible policies vis-à-vis the Germans. The French responded more quickly to the change as they moved to deepen the Franco-German relationship and the integration of the EC. British policy had to await the removal of Margaret Thatcher at the end of 1990 and the shift back toward Europe begun by John Major.

Poland

It is symbolic and portentous that Chancellor Kohl was in Warsaw on the day the Berlin Wall opened. He was meeting with Lech Walesa when the news came. Walesa turned to Kohl and expressed his belief that this would lead to German unification and that united Germany would give priority to itself at the expense of Poland. Poland would once again be the victim of history. Although Kohl reassured the Polish leader that this would not be the case, Horst Teltschik, who was present at the meeting, noted in his diary that he knew that Walesa was right.[245]

Poland came out of the process with both gains and losses. The major Polish gain was the German commitment to the Oder-Neisse border. The Poles were so sufficiently reassured by the border settlement and the guarantees of the Four Powers to maintain the agreement that they quickly lost interest in any further Soviet troop presence in Poland and pushed for their swift withdrawal. The reduction of military forces in eastern Germany also reassured the Poles, as did the limits on the size of the Bundeswehr and Germany's non-nuclear status.

Poland, however, as Walesa had foreseen, lost its priority for the Federal Republic. German resources flowed into eastern Germany and to the Soviet Union, and although Poland was the beneficiary of much German private investment, it undoubtedly would have received more assistance in the absence of these new German priorities.

The Polish-German relationship during the year of unification was also disquieting to many Poles. Unlike the conciliatory tones in which he addressed just about everyone else, Chancellor Kohl was notably cool, if not brusque, toward the Poles. The long debate over the Oder-Neisse border was unsettling, as was the pressure exerted on Poland in behalf of the German minority in Poland.

Yet Poland in the end looked toward Germany as the country that could modernize it. Most Poles understood that without German assistance, investment, know-how and goodwill, their transition to democracy and a mixed market economy would be much more hazardous. The German government also stressed reconciliation and held up the example of the Franco-German rapprochement as the model for the future of Polish-German relations.[246]

But the propinquity of a poor nation to a rich one will continue to nurture strains of envy, resentment and old stereotypes, not to mention the practical problems of immigration. Polish-East German relations were always bad, while those with the Federal Republic were markedly better. Which pattern will prevail after German unification is one of the key questions facing post-Cold War Europe.

UNITED GERMANY

The impact of unification on Germany is a topic that goes beyond the scope of this book and one that will surely be the subject of numerous articles and books for decades, if not centuries, to come, adding yet more volumes to the collection broadly entitled "The German Question." Yet an initial assessment will be offered nonetheless.

Comparing the outcome of the 2 + 4 process with the objectives the West Germans set out at its inception, it is clear that West Germany achieved what it set out to accomplish. Chancellor Kohl and Foreign Minister Genscher wished to achieve unification as quickly as possible with the goal of regaining full German sovereignty without being treated as a defeated nation. They wanted Germany to be treated as a "normal country" with the same rights and respect accorded France, Britain and other European states while avoiding a peace treaty and reparations.

In this important dimension the West Germans were completely successful. Germany emerged as a fully sovereign state on October 3, 1990. Although Soviet troops would remain on German soil until the end of 1994 at the latest, their status (and that of the Allied forces stationed in western Germany and Berlin) was no longer that of occupying forces or of units of a victor power. Reparations of any kind were also avoided, although individual claims against the former GDR were left open to adjudication.

The other major objective was for unification to occur within a stable European framework, to leave, in Genscher's words, "a European Germany, not a German Europe." Again, the West German agenda was achieved. The outstanding border questions were finally settled to the satisfaction of Germany's neighbors. Germany remained anchored in NATO and the European Community while NATO was transforming itself into an alliance that would be compatible with the new Europe.

German security was enhanced not only by maintaining membership within the Atlantic Alliance but also by the withdrawal of Soviet forces from eastern Germany and the dissolution of the Warsaw Pact. Germany was transformed from being a frontline state faced with the prospect of a short-warning attack launched by 380,000 Soviet forces stationed across the Elbe to a state that now had a buffer zone in Central Europe between itself and Russia. Its armed forces were limited to 370,000, a small number for a country of 76 million, and it remained denuclearized. The former GDR would not have foreign forces stationed on its territory and would be nuclear free, although it would have NATO-integrated Bundeswehr forces on its soil. The NATO security guarantee covered all of Germany. The trends both within Germany and in Europe were toward a downscaling of military forces and a broad demilitarization of foreign policy. In this sense the limitations on Germany were not disproportionate and could be reversed if a serious European crisis were to develop.

While West German objectives were fully realized, questions have been raised about those of the East Germans. The rapid unification of the country on West German terms caused serious problems of readjustment for the former East Germans. Resentment in the former GDR grew after unification over the domination of the new society by Western Germans. Many in the East came to feel like second-class citizens without their own identity. Everything associated with the GDR was discredited. There was no positive legacy. Many over 40 years of age felt that their lives had been wasted and that the changes that would come would be too late to help them.

In West Germany resentment also grew after the halcyon days of 1989 and 1990. Taxes and interest rates were increased to cover the mounting costs of reconstruction in the East. West Germans were faced with the growing problem of immigration, much of it from Eastern Europe. A general debate over the new German identity began, spurred in part by the divisive discussion over whether to move the capital from Bonn back to Berlin.

All this raised questions about whether the Kohl-Genscher approach to unification had been too rapid. Did it not undermine East German self-confidence and risk the destabilization of the West German economy? The answer to this question must be no. Given the circumstances of the time, the West German government did what had to be done. There is no convincing evidence that it artificially accelerated the process of unification for its own purposes. What in fact occurred was a massive and rapid collapse of the GDR between November 9, 1989, and mid-January 1990. The vast majority of East Germans wanted rapid unification, even if some East and West German intellectuals did not. There was no East German identity to support a separate nation. East Germany was the creation of the Soviet Union. It had no solid indigenous bases of legitimacy. It was a police state of massive proportions. All attempts by the communist leadership to evoke German themes and a German identity failed. East Germans identified Germany as the Federal Republic.

Once given the choice of reforming the GDR or joining the Federal Republic with its democracy and successful social market economy, the East Germans voted both with their feet and with their ballots for those parties who would bring unification as speedily as possible. The West German leadership was faced with a choice of shoring up a regime they abhorred, of closing the border to Germans or of giving hope to the East Germans with the prospect of rapid unification.

The West Germans were also dealing with a Soviet leadership that was the most reasonable one that could be hoped for, but one that was in serious trouble and could collapse at any moment to be replaced by a far different and less benign alternative. The developments that took place in the Soviet Union after unification seemed to justify the West German's rapid approach. The resignation of Shevardnadze in December 1990 took the leading Soviet architect of German unification out of the government and left a weakened Gorbachev facing a temporarily resurgent conservative opposition to his policies. It is unlikely that this regime would have been as reasonable as the one in which Shevardnadze shaped policy.

Life in unified Germany, despite the problems of unemployment and dislocation, was infinitely better for the people of the former GDR than it had been under the Stasi state. Civil liberties were restored, the economy was being rebuilt and people faced the future with hope, if not for themselves, then for their children. Even two years later, with all the problems they faced, the vast majority of Germans still believed that unification was good for themselves and for their country.

Finally, there are the multitude of questions opened for Europe by German unity. Would the new Germany destabilize the balance of power, unhinge the construction of the European Community and renationalize Europe? Would Germany turn back toward the East and *Mitteleuropa*? Would its reemergence as a sovereign nation lead it to become a Great Power, and would it fall once again into the megalomania that characterized its earlier attempts at European hegemony?

The future is open, and any attempts at providing answers in this dynamic and unpredictable context are likely to be futile and pointless. However, the new Germany is fundamentally different from that which Europe knew from 1871 to 1945. It is a democratic nation and is likely as a result to pursue foreign policies compatible with the constraints and values that operate in democratic polities. It has been unified in a Europe that has been undergoing a profound transformation since the formation of the European Community. Unified Germany, like West Germany, has proven to be "European" in its perspectives and policies, and if this remains the case, the prospect for a post national Europe will not be a utopian one. In this sense, the delayed unification of Germany during the Cold War gave Europe the time to begin to reorganize itself along integrationist lines, and the suddenness of German unification in 1990 provided an important impetus for rapid European union, of which the Maastricht summit of 1991 was an important step.

Finally the new Germany, unlike its predecessors, has a "German ideology" that stands for something more than mere power. The German model of a federal democracy and a social market economy that works is attractive not only to East Germans but to all of Europe and beyond. Its diplomacy, again in marked contrast to its twentieth century predecessors, is subtle, complex and constructive.

The role of the United States and the German-American relationship will be crucial in determining the shape of the new Europe. There are grounds for optimism here as well. The role the United States played in the diplomacy of German unification demonstrated its determination and ability to remain a European power as well as the closeness of the German-American partnership. Whether the two nations will emerge as "partners in leadership" remains an open but crucial question for Europe and the trans-Atlantic relationship.

The diplomacy of German unification began with the goals of avoiding a new Versailles and of establishing the conditions for a stable and democratic Europe. Its architects created the framework for a new Europe in which there are no losers and laid the foundations for an integrated and cooperative Euro-Atlantic system. It will be up to succeeding generations either to build upon this legacy or to squander it.

Appendix

TEXT OF TREATY ON THE FINAL SETTLEMENT
WITH RESPECT TO GERMANY

The Federal Republic of Germany, the German Democratic Republic, the French Republic, the Union of Soviet Socialist Republics, the United Kingdom of Great Britain and Northern Ireland and the United States of America,

Conscious of the fact that their peoples have been living together in peace since 1945;

Mindful of the recent historic changes in Europe which make it possible to overcome the division of the continent;

Having regarded to the rights and responsibilities of the Four Powers relating to Berlin and to Germany as a whole, and the corresponding wartime and post-war agreements and decisions of the Four Powers;

Resolved in accordance with their obligations under the Charter of the United Nations to develop friendly relations among nations based on respect for the principle of equal rights and self-determination of peoples, and to take other appropriate measures to strengthen universal peace;

Recalling the principles of the Final Act of the Conference on Security and Cooperation in Europe, signed in Helsinki;

Recognizing that those principles have laid firm foundations for the establishment of a just and lasting peaceful order in Europe;

Determined to take account of everyone's security interests;

Convinced of the need finally to overcome antagonism and to develop cooperation in Europe;

Confirming their readiness to reinforce security, in particular by adopting effective arms control, disarmament and confidence-building measures; their willingness not to regard each other as adversaries but to work for a relationship of trust and cooperation; and accordingly their readiness to consider positively setting up appropriate institutional arrangements within the framework of the Conference on Security and Cooperation in Europe;

Welcoming the fact that the German people, freely exercising their right of self-determination, have expressed their will to bring about the unity of Germany as a state so that they will be able to serve the peace of the world as an equal and sovereign partner in a united Europe;

Convinced that the unification of Germany as a state with definitive borders is a significant contribution to peace and stability in Europe;

Intending to conclude the final settlement with respect to Germany;

Recognizing that thereby, and with the unification of Germany as a democratic and peaceful state, the rights and responsibilities of the Four Powers relating to Berlin and to Germany as a whole lose their function;

Represented by their Ministers for Foreign Affairs who, in accordance with the Ottawa Declaration of February 13, 1990, met in Bonn on May 5, 1990, in Berlin on June 22, 1990, in Paris on July 17, 1990, with the participation of the Minister for Foreign Affairs of the Republic of Poland, and in Moscow on September 12, 1990;

Have agreed as follows:

ARTICLE 1

(1) The united Germany shall comprise the territory of the Federal Republic of Germany, the German Democratic Republic and the whole of Berlin. Its external borders shall be the borders of the Federal Republic of Germany and the German Democratic Republic and shall be definitive from the date on which the present Treaty comes into force. The confirmation of the definitive nature of the borders of the united Germany is an essential element of the peaceful order in Europe.

(2) The united Germany and the Republic of Poland shall confirm the existing border between them in a treaty that is binding under international law.

(3) The united Germany has no territorial claims whatsoever against other states and shall not assert any in the future.

(4) The Governments of the Federal Republic of Germany and the German Democratic Republic shall ensure that the constitution of the united Germany does not contain any provision incompatible with these principles. This applies accordingly to the provisions laid down in the preamble, the second sentence of Article 23, and Article 146 of the Basic Law for the Federal Republic of Germany.

(5) The Governments of the French Republic, the Union of Soviet Socialist Republics, the United Kingdom of Great Britain and Northern

Ireland and the United States of America take formal note of the corresponding commitments and declarations by the Governments of the Federal Republic of Germany and the German Democratic Republic and declare that their implementation will confirm the definitive nature of the united Germany's borders.

ARTICLE 2
The governments of the Federal Republic of Germany and the German Democratic Republic reaffirm their declarations that only peace will emanate from German soil. According to the constitution of the united Germany, acts tending to and undertaken with the intent to disturb the peaceful relations between nations, especially to prepare for aggressive war, are unconstitutional and a punishable offense. The governments of the Federal Republic of Germany and the German Democratic Republic declare that the united Germany will never employ any of its weapons except in accordance with its constitution and the Charter of the United Nations.

ARTICLE 3
(1) The Governments of the Federal Republic of Germany and the German Democratic Republic reaffirm their renunciation of the manufacture and possession of and control over nuclear, biological and chemical weapons. They declare that the united Germany, too, will abide by these commitments. In particular, rights and obligations arising from the Treaty on the Non-Proliferation of Nuclear Weapons of July 1, 1968, will continue to apply to the united Germany.

(2) The government of the Federal Republic of Germany, acting in full agreement with the Government of the German Democratic Republic, made the following statement on August 30, 1990, in Vienna at the Negotiations on Conventional Armed Forces in Europe:

"The Government of the Federal Republic of Germany undertakes to reduce the personnel strength of the armed forces of the united Germany to 370,000 (ground, air and naval forces) within three to four years. This reduction will commence on the entry into force of the first CFE agreement. Within the scope of this overall ceiling no more than 345,000 will belong to the ground and air forces which, pursuant to the agreed mandate, alone are the subject of the Negotiations on Conventional Armed Forces in Europe. The federal government regards its commitment to reduce ground and air forces as a significant German contribution to the reduction of conventional armed forces in Europe. It assumes that in follow-on negotiations the other participants in the negotiations, too, will render their contribution to enhancing security and stability in Europe, including measures to limit personnel strengths."

The government of the German Democratic Republic has expressly associated itself with this statement.

(3) The governments of the French Republic, the Union of Soviet Socialist Republics, the United Kingdom of Great Britain and Northern Ireland and the United States of America take note of these statements by the governments of the Federal Republic of Germany and the German Democratic Republic.

ARTICLE 4

(1) The governments of the Federal Republic of Germany, the German Democratic Republic and the Union of Soviet Socialist Republics state that the united Germany and the Union of Soviet Socialist Republics will settle by treaty the conditions for and the duration of the presence of Soviet armed forces on the territory of the present German Democratic Republic and of Berlin, as well as the conduct of the withdrawal of these armed forces which will be completed by the end of 1994, in connection with the implementation of the undertaking of the Federal Republic of Germany and the German Democratic Republic referred to in paragraph 2 of Article 3 of the present treaty.

(2) The governments of the French Republic, the United Kingdom of Great Britain and Northern Ireland and the United States of America take note of this statement.

ARTICLE 5

(1) Until the completion of the withdrawal of the Soviet armed forces from the territory of the present German Democratic Republic and of Berlin in accordance with Article 4 of the present treaty, only German territorial defense units which are not integrated into the alliance structures to which German armed forces in the rest of German territory are assigned will be stationed in that territory as armed forces of the united Germany. During that period and subject to the provisions of paragraph 2 of this Article, armed forces of other states will not be stationed in that territory or carry out any other military activity there.

(2) For the duration of the presence of Soviet armed forces in the territory of the present German Democratic Republic and of Berlin, armed forces of the French Republic, the United Kingdom of Great Britain and Northern Ireland and the United States of America will, upon German request, remain stationed in Berlin by agreement to this effect between the government of the united Germany and the governments of the states concerned. The

number of troops and the amount of equipment of all non-German armed forces stationed in Berlin will not be greater than at the time of signature of the present treaty. New categories of weapons will not be introduced there by non-German armed forces. The government of the united Germany will conclude with the governments of those states which have armed forces stationed in Berlin treaties with conditions which are fair taking account of the relations existing with the states concerned.

(3) Following the completion of the withdrawal of the Soviet armed forces from the territory of the present German Democratic Republic and of Berlin, units of German armed forces assigned to military alliance structures in the same way as those in the rest of German territory may also be stationed in that part of Germany, but without nuclear weapon carriers. This does not apply to conventional weapon systems which may have other capabilities in addition to conventional ones but which in that part of Germany are equipped for a conventional role and designated only for such. Foreign armed forces and nuclear weapons or their carriers will not be stationed in that part of Germany or deployed there.

ARTICLE 6
The right of the united Germany to belong to alliances, with all the rights and responsibilities arising therefrom, shall not be affected by the present treaty.

ARTICLE 7
(1) The French Republic, the Union of Soviet Socialist Republics, the United Kingdom of Great Britain and Northern Ireland and the United States of America hereby terminate their right and responsibilities relating to Berlin and to Germany as a whole. As a result, the corresponding, related quadripartite agreements, decisions and practices are terminated and all related Four Power institutions are dissolved.

(2) The united Germany shall have accordingly full sovereignty over its internal and external affairs.

ARTICLE 8
(1) The present treaty is subject to ratification or acceptance as soon as possible. On the German side it will be ratified by the united Germany. The treaty will therefore apply to the united Germany.

(2) The instruments of ratification or acceptance shall be deposited with the government of the united Germany. That government shall inform the governments of the other contracting parties of the deposit of each instrument of ratification or acceptance.

ARTICLE 9

The present Treaty shall enter into force for the united Germany, the French Republic, the Union of Soviet Socialist Republics, the United Kingdom of Great Britain and Northern Ireland and the United States of America on the date of deposit of the last instrument of ratification or acceptance by these states.

ARTICLE 10

The original of the present treaty, of which the English, French, German and Russian texts are equally authentic, shall be deposited with the government of the Federal Republic of Germany, which shall transmit certified true copies to the governments of the other contracting parties.

Agreed Minute To The Treaty On The Final Settlement With Respect To Germany Of September 12, 1990

Any questions with respect to the application of the word "deployed" as used in the last sentence of paragraph 3 of Article 5 will be decided by the government of the united Germany in a reasonable and responsible way taking into account the security interests of each contracting party as set forth in the preamble.

For the Federal Republic of Germany
Hans-Dietrich Genscher

For the German Democratic Republic
Lothar de Maizière

For the French Republic
Roland Dumas

For the Union of Soviet Socialist Republics
Eduard Shevardnadze

For the United Kingdom of Great Britain and Northern Ireland
Douglas Hurd

For the United States of America
James W. Baker III

Letter from Foreign Minister Hans-Dietrich Genscher (Federal Republic) and Prime Minister Lothar de Maizière (German Democratic Republic) to the foreign ministers of the United States, France, Great Britain and the Soviet Union, concerning the Treaty on the Final Settlement with Respect to Germany.

Mr. Foreign Minister,

In connection with the signing today of the Treaty on the Final Settlement with Respect to Germany, we would like to inform you that the governments of the Federal Republic of Germany and the German Democratic Republic declared the following in the negotiations:

1. The Joint Declaration of June 15, 1990, by the governments of the Federal Republic of Germany and the German Democratic Republic on the settlement of outstanding property matters contains, inter alia, the following observations:

"The expropriations effected on the basis of occupation law or sovereignty (between 1945 and 1949) are irreversible. The governments of the Soviet Union and the German Democratic Republic do not see any means of revising the measures taken then. The government of the Federal Republic of Germany takes note of this in the light of the historical development. It is of the opinion that a final decision on any public compensation must be reserved for a future all-German parliament."

According to Article 41 (1) of the treaty of August 31, 1990, between the Federal Republic of Germany and the German Democratic Republic establishing German unity (Unification Treaty), the aforementioned Joint Declaration forms an integral part of the Treaty. Pursuant to Article 41 (3) of the Unification Treaty, the Federal Republic of Germany will not enact any legislation contradicting the part of the Joint Declaration quoted above.

2. The monuments dedicated to the victims of war and tyranny which have been erected on German soil will be respected and will enjoy the protection of German law. The same applies to the war graves, which will be maintained and looked after.

3. In the united Germany, too, the free democratic basic order will be protected by the Constitution. It provides the basis for ensuring that parties, which, by reason of their aims or the behavior of their adherents, seek to impair or abolish the free democratic basic order as well as associations which are directed against the constitutional order or the concept of international understanding, can be prohibited. This also applies to parties and associations with National Socialist aims.

4. On the treaties of the German Democratic Republic, the following has been agreed in Article 12 (1) and (2) of the treaty of August 31, 1990, between

the Federal Republic of Germany and the German Democratic Republic establishing German unity:

"The contracting parties agree that, as part of the process of establishing German unity, the international treaties concluded by the German Democratic Republic shall be discussed with the contracting parties in terms of the protection of bona fide rights, the interests of the states concerned and the treaty obligations founded on the rule of law and taking into account the responsibilities of the European Communities in order to regulate or ascertain the continuance, adjustment or termination of such treaties.

"The united Germany shall lay down its position on the continuance of international treaties of the German Democratic Republic after consultations with the respective contracting parties and with the European Communities insofar as their responsibilities are affected."

Accept, Mr. Foreign Minister, the assurances of our high consideration.

NOTES

1. For a full discussion of the evolution of American policy on Germany in the postwar period see Frank A. Ninkovitch, *Germany and the United States: The Transformation of the German Question Since 1945* (Boston: Twayne, 1988).

2. See Wolfram Hanrieder, *Germany, America, Europe: Forty Years of German Foreign Policy* (New Haven: Yale University Press, 1989), pp. 133-40; and Anton DePorte, *Europe Between the Superpowers: The Enduring Balance* (New Haven: Yale University Press, 1979).

3. Hanrieder, *Germany, America, Europe*, p. 135.

4. John McCloy, quoted in Ninkovitch, *Germany and the United States*, p. 120.

5. In the words of an National Security Council memo written by Paul Nitze on July 30, 1952, "If the Free World acquires such strength, the internal contradictions of the Soviet totalitarian system will, with some positive assistance from us, cause that system gradually to weaken and decay." NSC 160/1 of August 17, 1953 argued that a united Europe would "exert a strong and increasing attraction on Eastern Europe, thus weakening the Soviet position there and accelerating Soviet withdrawal from that area." Both memos are cited by Ninkovitch, *Germany and the United States*, pp. 99 and 103.

6. See David P. Calleo, *Beyond American Hegemony: The Future of the Western Alliance* (New York: Basic Books, 1987), pp. 27 - 43; and John Lewis Gaddis, *Strategies of Containment: A Critical Appraisal of Postwar American National Security Policy* (New York: Oxford University Press, 1982), pp. 89-126.

7. Calleo, *Beyond American Hegemony*, p. 54.

8. Hanrieder coined and defined the phrase "double containment." See Hanrieder, *Germany, America, Europe*.

9. Memo to Acheson, January 6, 1959, cited in Ninkovitch, *Germany and the United States*, p. 83.

10. Renate Fritsch-Bournazel, " The Changing Nature of the German Question," in F. Stephen Larrabee, ed., *The Two German States and European Security* (New York: St. Martin's Press, 1989), p. 49.

11. Luigi Barzini, *The Europeans* (New York: Simon and Schuster, 1983), p. 70.

12. "Convention on Relations Between the Three Powers and the Federal Republic of Germany, May 26, 1952, As Amended by Schedule I of the Protocol on Termination of the Occupation Regime in Germany, Signed at Paris, October 23, 1954," in Office of the Historian, U.S. Department of State, *Documents*

on Germany 1944-1985, Department of State Publication 9446 (Washington, D.C.: undated), pp. 427-28.

13. Ronald Asmus, "Bonn and East Berlin: The Politics of German Unity and Partition," unpublished dissertation, Johns Hopkins University, 1991, p. 53.

14. See Christian Hacke, *Weltmacht wider Willen: Die Aussenpolitik der Bundesrepublik Deutschland* (Stuttgart: Klett Verlag, 1988), pp. 110-14.

15. Calleo, *Beyond American Hegemony,* p. 64.

16. Hanrieder, *German, America, Europe,* pp. 196-97.

17. See, for example, Henry Kissinger, *White House Years* (Boston: Little Brown, 1979), pp. 405-12; 529-34.

18. For a description and analysis of West German attitudes on arms control and détente in the 1980s, see Barry M. Blechman and Cathleen Fisher, eds., *The Silent Partner: West Germany and Arms Control* (Cambridge, Mass.: Ballinger, 1988).

19. See, for example, the series of opinion surveys sponsored by the Chicago Council on Foreign Relations, the most recent being John Reilly, ed., *American Public Opinion and U.S. Foreign Policy 1991* (Chicago: The Chicago Council on Foreign Relations, 1991), pp. 18-23.

20. A *New York Times* poll published in December 1989 found that 67 percent believed the two Germanies should be unified and only 16 percent believed that a unified Germany would try to dominate the world. *New York Times* (hereafter referred to as *NYT*), December 1, 1989, p. A21. See also *Business Week,* November 27, 1989, and *The Economist,* January 27, 1990, p. 49.

21. Quoted in David Hoffman, "Little Known Aide Plays Major Role in Foreign Policy," *Washington Post* (hereafter cited as *WP*), October 28, 1991, p. A 9. Hoffman also quotes from a 1980 article by Ross in *World Politics* in which Ross anticipated a breakdown in the Soviet elite consensus as the economy worsened.

22. Interview with author.

23. For an elaboration see Stanley R. Sloan, "The U.S. Role in a New World Order: Prospects for Bush's Global Vision," *CRS Report for Congress* (Washington, D.C.: Congressional Research Service, The Library of Congress, March 28, 1991), pp. 8-9.

24. See Dieter Buhl, "Vom Paten zum Partner Bonns," *Die Zeit* (North American ed., hereafter cited as *DZ*), July 27, 1990, p. 5. See also Michael H. Haltzel, "Amerikanische Einstellungen zur deutschen Wiedervereinigung," *Europa Archiv,* no. 4 (1990), pp. 127-132.

25. Speech by Hans-Dietrich Genscher, Minister for Foreign Affairs, in the German Bundestag, Bonn, April 27, 1989, *Statements and Speeches,* April 28, 1989 (New York: German Information Center), p. 2.

26. Timothy Garton Ash, "Germany Unbound," *The New York Review of Books,*

November 22, 1990, p. 11.

27. A survey and analysis of German public opinion both in the East and in the West conducted by the Rand Corporation in October 1990 found that when asked to rank how important the following factors were in contributing to the demise of the SED regime, 75 percent of West Germans and 73 percent of East Germans listed Gorbachev's policies as very large in this regard, compared with only 18 percent of West Germans and 15 percent of East Germans who listed the resolute stance of the Western alliance as a very large factor; 19 percent of the West Germans and 26 percent of the East Germans credited *Ostpolitik* as a very large factor. After Gorbachev, regime opposition groups in the DDR and in Poland and Hungary were listed as large factors (42 to 56 percent in the former case and 31 to 44 percent in the latter). Fifty-nine percent of West Germans, however, agreed with the statement that the stationing of American troops in the FRG and Berlin contributed to the overcoming of the division of Germany, but only 33 percent of East Germans agreed with this assessment. See Ronald Asmus, *German Perceptions of the United States on the Eve of Unification* (Santa Monica, Calif.: The Rand Corporation, January 1991), figures 12 and 13.

28. This is a point made as well by Timothy Garton-Ash who distinguishes between "the passive and the active influence of the Federal Republic: that which it exerts by virtue of its mere existence, freedom, prosperity, and that which it exerts by virtue of deliberate policy (that is *Deutschlandpolitik*). The former is arguably larger in influence than the latter." *"Mitteleuropa?"* *Daedalus* 119, no. 1 (Winter 1990), p. 15.

29. For details of the extent of this dependency, see Jonathan Dean, *Watershed in Europe: Dismantling the East-West Military Confrontation* (Lexington, Mass.: Lexington Books, 1987), pp. 237-256.

30. Horst Teltschik, *329 Tage: Innenansichten der Einigung* (Berlin: Siedler, 1991), p. 28.

31. Quoted by Thomas Friedman and Michael R. Gordon, "Steps to German Unity: Bonn as a Power," *NYT,* February 16, 1990, p. A9.

32. Teltschik, *329 Tage,* p. 320.

33. Robert Leicht, "Das Gute Klima nutzen," *DZ,* April 13, 1990. That this rapport originated during the SNF negotiations was confirmed in interviews with U.S. officials.

34. Christopher Madison, "Baker's Inner Circle," *National Journal,* July 13, 1991, p. 1734. See also Don Oberdorfer, *The Turn: From the Cold War to a New Era—The United States and the Soviet Union, 1983-1990* (New York: Poseidon Press, 1991), pp. 335-36.

35. Interview with the author, January 1992.

36. As one commentator noted, this division of labor has discouraged the best and the brightest in the CDU from entering the foreign policy arena. "The main reason is that few want to move into a field where the scope of influence

is so limited. This is surprising in view of the CDU and CSU tradition. What is more it is a dangerous development in a country such as the Federal Republic of Germany, where foreign policy is perhaps more significant than in any other European country." Völker Jacobs, "CDU's Subordinate Role in Foreign Affairs Analyzed," *Saarbrücker Zeitung*, April 30, 1988, translated and reprinted in *The German Tribune*, May 15, 1988, p. 3.

37. Nina Gruneberg, "Der richtige Riecher: Helmut Kohl, Kanzler der Einheit," *DZ*, October 5, 1990, p.3.

38. Kohl is reported by his close aide Konrad Seiters to have had an "awakening" (*Erweckungserlebnis*) during his first trip to Dresden on December 19, 1989. After experiencing the warm welcome of tens of thousands of East Germans in the streets and hearing chants of "*Deutschland einig Vaterland*" (Germany one fatherland) he turned to Seiters and said, "*Seiters, es ist gelaufen*" (Seiters, it has happened). Grunenberg, "Der richtige Riecher," p. 3.

39. As reported by Teltschik, *329 Tage*, p. 320.

40. Vyacheslav Dashichev, in comments at a seminar held at the American Institute for Contemporary German Studies, Johns Hopkins University, Washington, D.C., July 17, 1991.

41. Interview with Soviet Foreign Ministry official, January 1992.

42. Oberdorfer, *The Turn*, p. 336.

43. See, for example, Don Oberdorfer, "Baker's Evolution at State," *WP*, November 16, 1989, p. A1, A43; and Madison, "Baker's Inner Circle."

44. Quoted in Madison, "Baker's Inner Circle," p. 1738.

45. "The truth is that Mr. Baker, who was a great manager for Mr. Reagan, is unable to complement Mr. Bush in this (public) area. While the President feels no need to explain his policies to the public, the frosty Mr. Baker cannot compensate because he hates politicking and engaging with the public." Maureen Dowd with Thomas L. Friedman, "Could Baker's Grip on Tiller Right Bush Campaign Drift," *NYT*, March 29, 1992, p. 14.

46. Interview with author.

47. See John E. Osborn, "On the Reunification of Germany," *American Journal of International Law* 86, no. 2 (April 1992), pp. 343-45.

48. This point was confirmed by Richard Kiessler, diplomatic correspondent of *Der Spiegel*, in his comments at a seminar of the American Institute for Contemporary German Studies, Johns Hopkins University, Washington, D.C., January 24, 1992. These strains and animosity toward Genscher are apparent to the reader of Teltschik's book, *329 Tage*.

49. For more on Teltschik see Christoph Bertram, "Ausstieg eines Seitenein-steigers," *DZ*, December 21, 1990, p. 5.

50. See Friedman and Gordon, "Steps to German Unity," and John Newhouse, "The Diplomatic Round: Sweeping Change," *New Yorker*, August 27, 1990, p. 85.

51. As reported by Wolfgang Schäuble, *Der Vertrag: Wie ich über die deutsche Einheit verhandelte* (Stuttgart: Deutsche Verlags Anstalt, 1991), p. 130.

52. "Wir haben dort mitzureden," *Der Spiegel,* no. 13 (March 26, 1990), p. 19. Teltschik recounts de Maizière's interview with a West German newspaper shortly after the opening of the Wall in which he said that he "held socialism for one of the most beautiful visions of human thought," and added, "If you believe that the demands for democracy also mean a demand for the deconstruction of socialism, then you must understand that we have different views." Teltschik writes, "This interview fed our scepticism about de Maizière further." Teltschik, *329 Tage,* pp. 38-9.

53. The lack of a significant role for the East Germans in 2 + 4 is confirmed by interviews and by Karl Kaiser, "Germany's Unification," *Foreign Affairs, America and the World 1990/91* 70, no. 1 (Winter 1991), p. 187.

54. "Genscher und Meckel wollen die Aussenpolitik auf allen Gebieten koordinieren," *Frankfurter Allgemeine Zeitung* (hereafter cited as *FAZ*), April 26, 1990.

55. For a thorough account of Soviet policy toward East Germany under Gorbachev up to the opening of the Wall, see Jeffrey Gedmin, *The Hidden Hand: Gorbachev and the Collapse of East Germany* (Washington, D.C.: The American Enterprise Institute, 1992).

56. Karl Kaiser, *Deutschlands Vereinigung: Die internationale Aspekte* (Bergische Gladbach: Bastei Luebbe, 1991), p. 21.

57. This classification is a modification of that offered by Pauline Neville-Jones, Minister, British Embassy, Bonn during this period. Minister Jones offered a tripartite taxonomy that divided the process into the revolution on the ground (September-November or later), the conceptual phase (January-February, 1990) and a negotiating phase (April-July). "Seminar with Pauline Neville-Jones," The American Institute for Contemporary German Studies, Johns Hopkins University, Washington, D.C., May 21, 1991.

58. F. Stephen Larrabee, "The View From Moscow," in F. Stephen Larrabee, ed., *The Two German States and European Security* (New York: St. Martin's Press, 1989), p. 182.

59. Ibid., pp. 184-86.

60. See Michael J. Sodaro, *Moscow, Germany and the West From Khrushchev to Gorbachev* (Ithaca, N.Y.: Cornell University Press, 1990), pp. 265-326; and Larrabee, "The View From Moscow," pp. 189- 203.

61. Hannes Adomeit, "Soviet Perspectives on Tomorrow's Germany," in Gary Geipel, ed., *The Future of Germany* (Indianapolis, Ind.: The Hudson Institute, 1990), p. 168. See also Gedmin, *The Hidden Hand.*

62. For more on the reorientation of Soviet security policy, see Sodaro, *Moscow, Germany and the West,* pp. 326-335.

63. Adomeit, "Soviet Perspectives," p. 168.

64. Comments at a seminar held at the American Institute for Contemporary German Studies, Johns Hopkins University, Washington, D.C., July 17, 1991. For a good survey of the Soviet discussion on the German Question just prior to the German Revolution see Sodaro, *Moscow, Germany and the West,* pp. 352-364; and Gedmin, *The Hidden Hand.*

65. Horst Teltschik, presentation to a seminar group at the American Institute for Contemporary German Studies, Johns Hopkins University, Washington, D.C., November 26, 1991. Kohl followed up on this promise and provided Hungary with assurances that it would make up for any losses in oil deliveries from the Soviet Union when he was visited by Nemeth ten days after the Wall opened. See Teltschik, *329 Tage,* pp. 39-40. For a Hungarian version of the events leading to the release of the East Germans into Austria see Gyula Horn, *Freiheit die ich meine: Erinnerungen des ungarischen Aussenministers, der den Eisernen Vorhang oeffnete* (Hamburg: Hoffmann und Campe, 1991), pp. 308-333.

66. Interview with the author, January 1992.

67. Based on interviews conducted in January 1992 with two Soviet officials who were in key positions in the Foreign Ministry during November 1989.

68. On November 9, 1989, the West German Interior Ministry announced that the number of East Germans leaving the GDR for the FRG *(Übersiedler)* during 1989 was 225,233, of which 48,177 came after the opening of the border with Czechoslovakia on November 3. By the end of 1989 the total had risen to 343,854. Eleanor Baumann, et al., *Der Fischer Weltalmanach Sonderband DDR* (Frankfurt: Fischer Taschenbuch Verlag, April 1990), pp. 134, 142.

69. Interview with German Foreign Ministry official, June 1991.

70. Teltschik, *329 Tage,* pp. 42-45.

71. Teltschik also adds a few other names to this list. See Teltschik, *329 Tage,* p. 49-50.

72. "Im Bundestag kommt Streit auf über die Deutschlandpolitik," *FAZ,* November 30, 1989, p. 1; Udo Bergdoll, "Zehn Stufen auf einem langen Weg," *Süddeutsche Zeitung* (hereafter cited as *SZ*), November 29, 1989; and "Ein Staatenbund? Ein Bundesstaat?" *Der Spiegel,* no. 49 (December 4, 1989), pp. 24-29.

73. Horst Schreitter, "Ruf nach Wiederbelebung," *Frankfurter Rundschau* (hereafter cited as *FR*), November 15, 1989, p. 2. Genscher rejected the proposal on the grounds that only after a process of continuing rapprochement between the two German states was a peace treaty possible. The SPD leadership also distanced itself from Bahr's call, arguing that the reform process in the GDR should not be burdened by a connection to reunification.

74. Interview with aides in Chancellor's office, June 1991. Brandt sensed the momentum toward unification very early and the week before the Ten Point Plan was announced, he said, "Unity is growing up from the people in a way

that hardly anyone has foreseen." "Der Druck von unten wächst," *Der Spiegel,* no. 48 (November 27, 1989), p. 18.

75. Ibid., p. 16.

76. Teltschik recounts this motivation in the discussions leading up to the Ten Point Plan. "This evening (November 20) we are unanimous that the high international reputation of the Chancellor must be used more strongly in domestic politics and that the German question could serve as a bridge for a better image of the Chancellor." Teltschik, *329 Tage,* p. 41.

77. This assessment is based on interviews with officials by the author in the Chancellor's office. Teltschik's view was that he was thinking at this time in terms of a five-to-ten-year time period. See Teltschik, *329 Tage,* p. 52.

78. Ibid., p. 50.

79. Marc Fisher, "Kohl Proposes Broad Program for Reunification of Germany," *WP,* November 29, 1989, p. A33.

80. Ibid., p. A1.

81. "Der Druck von unten waechst," p. 16.

82. Ibid., p. 15.

83. Comments made at a seminar at the American Institute for German Studies, Johns Hopkins University, Washington, D.C., May 21, 1991.

84. Jim Hoagland, "The End of the Special Relationship," *WP,* December 7, 1989, p. A27.

85. Haltzel, "Amerikanische Einstellungen," p. 129.

86. James Baker III, "A New Europe, A New Atlanticism: Architecture for a New Europe," *Current Policy,* no. 1233, Washington, D.C.: Department of State, December 12, 1989.

87. Excerpts of the Baker speech can be found in *WP,* December 13, 1989, p. A28.

88. The precondition of NATO membership was viewed by some as "an unfulfillable condition" and evidence of U.S. opposition to reunification. See "Ein Staatenbund? Ein Bundesstaat?" *Der Spiegel,* no. 49 (December 4, 1989), p. 25.

89. See Peter R. Weilemann, "The German Contribution Toward Overcoming the Division of Europe—Chancellor Helmut Kohl's 10 Points," *Aussenpolitik,* no. 1 (1990), p. 22.

90. "Die Siegermächte warnen Bonn," *Der Spiegel,* no. 50 (December 11, 1989), p. 17.

91. David Remnick, "Soviets Attack West German Proposal on Reunification," *WP,* November 30, 1989, p. A53.

92. Michael Dobbs, "Soviet Leader Backs German Links, Rejects Changes in Postwar Borders," *WP,* December 2, 1989, p. A24.

93. "Der Druck von unten wächst," p. 15.

94. Quoted in Jackson Diehl and John Goshko, "4 Powers Stress 'Importance of Stability' Amid German Change," *WP*, December 12, 1989, p. A38.

95. See Dominic Lawson, "Saying the Unsayable about the Germans," *The Spectator*, July 14, 1990, pp. 8-10.

96. Kaiser, *Deutschlands Vereinigung*, p. 65.

97. Diehl and Goshko, "4 Powers," p. A38.

98. "London: Bedenken nach unerwartetem Wandel," *FAZ*, December 15, 1989. For a report on the British press reaction to the Ten Point Plan see "Grossbritannien: Thatcher: Erst demokratisiern," *FR*, November 30, 1989.

99. This point was made by Pauline Neville-Jones, Minister of the British Embassy in Bonn during the unification period in remarks delivered at a seminar at the American Institute for Contemporary German Studies, Johns Hopkins University, Washington, D.C., on May 21, 1991.

100. See Kaiser, *Deutschlands Vereinigung*, pp. 65-66.

101. A poll conducted in France the week after the opening of the Berlin Wall found that two-thirds had feelings of good will toward the Germans and only 17 percent expressed either fear or hostility. More than 60 percent did not fear the prospect of a unified Germany and 86 percent agreed that reunification would be a good thing for Germany while 70 percent said it would be good for the EEC. "Dumas on Gorbachev Meeting, German Reunification," Paris, AFP reprinted in Foreign Broadcast Information Service, *West Europe Report* (hereafter cited as *FBIS-WE*), November 16, 1980, p. 18.

102. Comments made by Dominique Moisi at a seminar held at the American Institute for Contemporary German Studies, Johns Hopkins University, Washington, D.C., on June 4, 1991.

103. See David Yost, "France in the New Europe," *Foreign Affairs* 69, no. 5 (Winter 1990/91), p. 111.

104. See Peter Riddell and David Buchan, "NATO agrees in its approach to German reunification," *The Financial Times* (hereafter cited as *FT*), December 5, 1989, p. 2.

105. "Die Siegermächte warnen Bonn," p. 17.

106. Newhouse, "The Diplomatic Round," p. 81.

107. "Bonn/Paris: Splitter im Körper," *Der Spiegel*, no. 1, January 1, 1990, p. 26. This article goes on to misreport that the French had gotten American support to block a unified German state.

108. Jim Hoagland, "Germans and French," *WP*, December 14, 1989, p. A31.

109. For a summary of the French response to German unification in the early stages of the collapse of the GDR see Walter Schütze, "Frankreich angesichts der deutschen Einheit," *Europa Archiv* (February 25, 1990), pp. 133-38; reprinted in "Course of French Response to Unification Traced," *FBIS-WE*,

June 15, 1990, Annex, p. 1-5; Anne Marie LeGloannec, "Change in German and Future West European Security Arrangements" in Gary Geipel, ed., *The Future of Germany* (Indianapolis, Ind.: The Hudson Institute, 1990), pp. 129-139; and " French Fears Surface With Polish Border Issue," *Neue Züricher Zeitung,* March 14, 1990, reprinted in *FBIS-WE,* April 24, 1990, Annex, p. 3.

110. Oberdorfer, *The Turn,* p. 393.

111. President Richard von Weizsäcker made these points early when he declared that the German question could only be solved as part of a larger process of European unification. See "Kein deutscher Sonderweg in Europa," *SZ,* January 10, 1990.

112. "Bundeskanzler legt Drei Stufen-Plan für Weg zur Wiedervereinigung vor," *Die Welt,* November 28, 1990.

113. Elizabeth Pond, *After the Wall* (New York: Priority Press, 1990), p. 41.

114. Klaus Gotto, "Der Realist Als Visionär," *Die Politische Meinung,* no. 249 (March/April 1990), pp. 10-11.

115. The following quotes are taken from "German Unity within the European Framework," speech by Foreign Minister Hans-Dietrich Genscher at a conference at the Tutzing Protestant Academy, January 31, 1990, *Statements and Speeches* 13, no. 2 (New York: German Information Center, February 6, 1990).

116. Ibid., p.3.

117. Rühe stated on February 3, "In a united Europe there is no space for neutrality. We are on the side of the democracies. However the stage of security will change in the European home. The old alliances will assume new roles. The military structure of NATO will neither be extended to the Oder River, nor will the present role of NATO in terms of security policy remain unchanged in a unified Germany." "CDU's Rühe on Modrow Plan, German Unity," *Bild,* February 3, 1990, pp. 1, 3 and reprinted in *FBIS-WE,* February 6, 1990, p. 7. Stoltenberg placed continuing emphasis upon the NATO treaty extending to all of Germany and of German forces remaining in the integrated military command, although NATO forces would not be deployed into the territory of the GDR. Territorial forces not under NATO command would be deployed in this region. Stephan-Andreas Casdorff, "NATO Schutz soll für ganz Deutschland gelten," *SZ,* February 17/18, 1990, p. 1.

118. Interview with author, June 1991.

119. Friedman and Gordon, "Steps to German Unity," p. A9.

120. Quoted in "Washington und Moskau reagieren positiv auf Genschers Vorschläge zum NATO Bereich," *SZ,* February 9, 1990, p. 1.

121. From an interview with NSC official, June 1991.

122. From an interview with aide in the Chancellor's office, June 1991.

123. Quoted by Oberdorfer, *The Turn*, p. 395.

124. Quoted in ibid., p. 396. See also Friedman and Gordon, "Steps to German Unity," p. A9.

125. Interview with the author August, 1991.

126. "Press Conference, The Honorable James Baker, Secretary of State Following US-USSR Ministerial Meetings, Novosti Press Center, Moscow, USSR, February 9, 1990" (Washington, D.C.: U.S. Department of State, PR No. 14, February 16, 1990), p. 5.

127. As reported in "Wir müssen es behutsam tun," *Der Spiegel*, no. 8, February 19, 1990, p. 17.

128. Udo Bergdoll and Bernhard Küppers, "Kohl: Die Weg zur deutschen Einheit ist frei" *SZ*, February 12, 1990, p. 1.

129. Quoted in "Wir müssen es behutsam tun," p. 17.

130. Ibid., p. 17.

131. Ibid., p. 18.

132. "Kohl statement on Gorbachev Talks," *Die Welt*, February 12, 1990, p. 4 and reprinted in *FBIS-WE*, February 12, 1990, p. 6.

133. "Bonner Schlüssel," *Der Spiegel*, no. 9, February 26, 1990, p. 20.

134. Ibid., p. 20.

135. Friedman and Gordon, "Steps to German Unity," p. A9.

136. From Friedman and Gordon, "Steps to German Unity," p. 19; confirmed in interview with official in German Foreign Office, June 1991.

137. "Bonner Schlüssel," p. 21.

138. Quoted later by Serge Schmemann, "A Normal Germany," *NYT*, December 4, 1990, p. A20.

139. "Nicht den Buchhaltern überlassen," *Der Spiegel*, no. 20, May 14, 1990, p. 28.

140. Paul E. Gallis, *The Unification of Germany: Background and Analysis of the Two-Plus-Four Talks* (Washington, D.C.: Congressional Research Service, U.S. Library of Congress, April 16, 1990), pp. 24-27.

141. Robert Leicht, "Das gute Klima nutzen," *Die Zeit*, April 4, 1990. See also "Wie man die Einheit politisch einbettet," *SZ*, February 20, 1990, for a description on the inner-party debate on security alternatives and unity and the *Spiegel* interview with Genscher, "Nicht den Buchhaltern überlassen."

142. See, for example, the statements of Vitale Churkin as quoted in Leo Wieland, "In Moskau bedarf es einer Denkpause-Tschurkin hin, Tschurkin her," *FAZ*, February 14, 1990.

143. "Bizarres Szenario," *Der Spiegel*, no. 7, February 12, 1990.

144. See "Enormer Schaden für Moskau," *Der Spiegel*, no. 6, February 5, 1990,

pp. 142-58.

145. Gallis, *The Unification of Germany*, p. 29.

146. Interview with State Department official, August 1991.

147. Gallis, *The Unification of Germany*, p. 24.

148. Interview with National Security Council official, June 1991.

149. "Weit weg von Aussöhnung," *Der Spiegel*, no. 45, November 6, 1989, p. 19.

150. "Kohl, Bush: Full NATO Membership for a United Germany," *The Week in Germany* (New York: German Information Center, March 2, 1990), p. 1; Pond, *After the Wall*, pp. 55-8; and Robert Pear, "Bush and Kohl Try to Allay Fears Of a Reunified Germany's Powers," *NYT*, February 26, 1990, p. A1.

151. "FDP lehnt Kohls Forderungen an Polen ab—Genscher will Kanzler zur Korrektur bewegen," *SZ*, March 5, 1990, p. 1.

152. "Polen wird an 2 + 4 Gesprächen beteiligt," *FAZ*, March 15, 1990.

153. "Kohl: Currency Treaty, Border Resolution Are Steps Toward Unity," *The Week in Germany* (New York: German Information Center, June 22, 1990), p. 1.

154. "Two Germanies Vow to Accept Poland's Postwar Frontiers," *NYT*, July 18, 1990, p. A6.

155. Stephen Kinzer, "Germans and Poles Pledge Mutual Help," *NYT*, June 18, 1991, p. A3.

156. Marc Fisher, "Kohl Promises Polish Border Treaty Now," *WP*, November 9, 1990, p. A20.

157. The election results were: Alliance for Germany (CDU and allied parties) 48.2 percent, SPD 21.8 percent, PDS (Communists) 16.3 percent, FDP 5.3 percent, Alliance 90, 2.9 percent.

158. "Bonn weist Moskauer Einwände gegen Staatsvertrag zurück," *FAZ*, April 21, 1990.

159. "Kritische Gemütslage," *Der Spiegel*, no. 13, March 26, 1990, p. 25.

160. Jim Hoagland, "The Shevardnadze Surprise," *WP*, August 1, 1991, p. A15.

161. "Teltschik Comments on Two-Plus-Four Talks," Hamburg DPA, May 7, 1990, in *FBIS-WE*, May 8, 1990, p. 6.

162. For a good account of Soviet policy toward the GDR in 1989, see Fred Oldenburg, "Sowjetische Deutschland-Politik nach der Oktober Revolution in der DDR," *Deutschland Archiv* 23 (January 1990), pp. 68-76.

163. Quoted in Newhouse, "The Diplomatic Round," p. 82.

164. Christoph Bertram, "Ein Weltrekord der Diplomaten," *DZ*, September 14, 1990, p. 4.

165. Newhouse, "The Diplomatic Round," p. 85.

166. Interview with German Foreign Ministry official, June 1991.

167. "Shevardnadze Delivers Speech," *Foreign Broadcast Information Service—Soviet Union* (hereafter *FBIS-SOV*) 90-088, May 7, 1990, p. 5.

168. Ibid., p. 5. Later in the same speech the Soviet Foreign Minister came back to this point forcefully, saying, "The population of our country, having borne such terrible losses in the last war, irreconcilably regards the idea of including a united Germany in NATO. This has again been shown by an opinion poll which was recently carried out throughout the whole country. There are such moods in our Supreme Soviet as well. We cannot but take this into consideration. . . . I would ask colleagues to understand that we are neither playing nor bluffing here."

169. Ibid., p. 6.

170. See "Wendemarke der Geschichte?" *Der Spiegel*, no. 20, May 14, 1990, p. 19.

171. Teltschik, *329 Tage*, p. 224.

172. "Secret Bonn-Moscow Financial Talks Reported," *FBIS-WE*, May 21, 1990, pp. 7-8. John Newhouse, in his account, reported that the German embassy in Moscow was unaware of Teltschik's visit but this is not supported by the German policymakers interviewed by the author. In general, journalistic accounts seem to have exaggerated the differences between the Chancellor's Office and the Foreign Office. See Newhouse, "The Diplomatic Round," p. 85.

173. For Teltschik's account, see *329 Tage*, pp. 230-5.

174. See "Summit 'Movement' Expected," *Handelsblatt*, May 30, 1990, p. 8 and reprinted in FBIS-WE, May 30, 1990, p. 4; and "Genscher Urges Changes in Alliances' Relationship," DPA, May 31, 1990, in FBIS-WE, May 31, 1990, p. 6.

175. Teltschik, *329 Tage*, pp. 238-39.

176. Thomas Friedman, "U.S. Will Press the Soviets to Accept Plan on Germany," *NYT*, June 5, 1990, p. A17.

177. Ibid.

178. Thomas L. Friedman, "Wide Differences Over Germany Are Still Said to Divide the Superpowers," *NYT*, June 2, 1990, p. 7.

179. R. Jeffrey Smith, "Conventional Arms Pact, Germany Question Tied," *WP*, June 4, 1990, p. 18.

180. Edward Cody, "Bonn Says Reunification is Eased," *WP*, June 4, 1990, p. A17. See also the comments of Kohl and Genscher as reported in *FBIS-WE*, June 4, 1990, pp. 8-9.

181. "Viele Überraschungen," *Der Spiegel*, no. 26, June 25, 1990, p.18.

182. R. Jeffrey Smith, "Power Shift Presages the Future Germany," *WP*, July 6, 1990, p. 28.

183. "Nicht den Buchhaltern überlassen," p. 29.

184. Ibid.

185. In the case of Britain after Suez, as David French observes, "Macmillan and his colleagues in 1957 were no more ready than Atlee and his colleagues had been in 1945 to abandon their conviction that Britain was still a great power. Their solution to the problem of how to meet Britain's security needs and spend a smaller proportion of national resources on defense was to acquire an independent strategic deterrent." David French, "Britain and NATO: Past, Present and Future," Paper for the Core Seminar Series on NATO at Forty, Woodrow Wilson International Center for Scholars, Washington, D.C., February 27, 1989, p. 6. As for France, "Following the humiliation of the German occupation and then the loss of Indo-China, nuclear weapons were seen as a possible aid to national recovery, boosting morale and ensuring that France returned to her proper rank amongst the nations." Lawrence Freedman, *The Evolution of Nuclear Strategy* (New York: St. Martin's Press, 1989), p. 313.

186. Harold MacMillan spoke in 1958 of how the independent deterrent "gives us a better position in the world, it gives us a better position with respect to the United States. It puts us where we ought to be, in the position of a Great Power. The fact that we have it makes the United States pay a greater regard to our point of view, and that is of great importance." Television interview of February 1958 cited in Andrew Pierre, *Nuclear Politics: The British Experience with an Independent Strategic Force, 1939-1970* (London: Oxford University Press, 1972), p. 178.

187. French, "Britain and NATO," p. 10.

188. Bundeswehr General Inspector Wellershof, for example, stated in April 1988, "The history of war is . . . the history of the failure of purely conventional deterrence." Interview with *SZ*, April 9/10, 1988, p. 11. This sentiment was also voiced by Margaret Thatcher during the April 1989 visit of Mikhail Gorbachev to London. She stated in a dinner speech, "Both our countries know from bitter experience that conventional weapons do not deter war in Europe, whereas nuclear weapons have done so for over forty years." Quoted in "Gorbachev Criticizes Lack of U.S. Policy," *WP*, April 7, 1989, p. 14.

189. Smith, "Power Shift Presages The Future Germany," p. 28; Michael Gordon, "Nuclear Strategy Shift?" *NYT*, July 3, 1990, p. 1; Jim Hoagland, "Last Resort Policy Posed for A-Arms," *WP*, July 2, 1990, p. 1.

190. NATO Press Service, *London Declaration On A Transformed North Atlantic Alliance* (Brussels, July 6, 1990), p. 5.

191. Michael Gordon, "A New Face For NATO," *NYT*, July 8, 1990, p. 6.

192. Eberhard Wisdorff, "Der Gipfel der Allianz schuf die Voraussetzung für Gorbatschows Zustimmung," *Handelsblatt*, July 18, 1990.

193. "Eine Frage der Würde," *Der Spiegel*, no. 27, July 2, 1990, p.18.

194. Ibid., p. 19.

195. Interview with Soviet Foreign Ministry official, January 1992.

196. Bill Keller, "Shevardnadze Says Moves Pave Way to 'a Safe Future' for Europe," *NYT*, July 7, 1990, p. 1. Foreign Ministry Spokesman Gerasimov said, "Now we can tell them [the hard-liners] that they are wrong."

197. Interview with the author, January 1992.

198. "PRAVDA Carries 3 July Speeches, Reports: Foreign Minister Shevardnadze," *FBIS-SOV* 90-130-S, July 6, 1990, p. 48.

199. Ibid.

200. Ibid., pp. 48-9.

201. Ibid., p. 49.

202. For Shevardnadze's comments before the Supreme Soviet, see "Shevardnadze Addresses Panel on German Treaty," *FBIS-SOV* 90-184, September 21, 1990, pp. 20-1.

203. Interview with the author, January 1992.

204. Quoted in Hans Klein, *Es begann im Kaukasus* (Berlin: Ullstein, 1991), p. 87. Also cited by Teltschik, *329 Tage*, p. 325.

205. Teltschik, *329 Tage*, p. 310.

206. See Bill Keller, "Gorbachev Yields on Alliance Roles in a New Germany," *NYT*, June 13, 1990, p. A1; Thomas Friedman, "Gorbachev Said to Ease on Germany in NATO," *NYT*, June 13, 1990, p. A18; and, Ferdinand Protzman, "Bonn Welcomes New Soviet Shift," *NYT*, June 14, 1990, p. A17.

207. Interview with Soviet Foreign Ministry official, January 1992.

208. The only public written account of this meeting is that provided by Teltschik, *329 Tage*, pp. 319-32. Another participant in the broader discussions in the Caucasus who has published his recollection of the events was Hans Klein, the Chancellor's Press secretary in his book, *Es begann im Kaukasus*. The account of these meetings which follows relies on these sources, other journalistic accounts and interviews with other German officials, including one who was a participant at the meeting.

209. Teltschik, *329 Tage*, p. 323.

210. Olaf Ihlau, "Das gewaltige Gefühl der Erleichterung," *SZ*, July 18, 1990, p. 3. See also Teltschik, *329 Tage*, p. 319-20.

211. Klein, *Es begann im Kaukasus*, p. 72.

212. Interview with German Foreign Ministry official, June 1991.

213. "Die Hoffnung heisst Germanija," *Der Spiegel*, no. 30, July 23, 1990, pp. 17-8.

214. As he told Hans Klein the next day. See Klein, *Es begann im Kaukasus*, p. 250.

215. Quoted in "Wir müssen es behutsam tun," p. 18.

216. "Bonner Schlüssel," p. 21.

217. In discussions of the Genscher Plan, Stoltenberg placed continuing emphasis upon the NATO treaty extending to all of Germany and of German forces remaining in the integrated military command, although NATO forces would not be deployed on the territory of the GDR. Territorial forces not under NATO command would be deployed in this region. In this article it was also falsely reported that Stoltenberg supported the stationing of Allied troops in the former GDR. See Casdorff, "NATO Schutz soll für ganz Deutschland gelten," p. 1.

218. "Genscher: Bundeswehr nicht auf DDR-Gebiet," *SZ*, February 19, 1990, p. 1.

219. See *Pressemitteilung*, no. 74/90, February 19, 1990 (Bonn: Presse und Informationsamt der Bundesregierung, typed). See also "Koalitionsstreit um Geltungsbereich der NATO in vereinigten Deutschland vorest beigelegt," *SZ*, February 20, 1990, p. 1.

220. "Kritische Gemütslage," *Der Spiegel*, no. 13, March 26, 1990, p. 25.

221. "Die Hoffnung heisst Germanija," p. 17. Other sources on the German discussion on force limits are interviews conducted by the author and Teltschik's, *329 Tage*, pp. 291-96.

222. Klein, *Es begann im Kaukasus*, p. 261.

223. "Excerpts From Kohl-Gorbachev News Conference," *NYT*, July 17, 1990, p. A8; See also Serge Schmemann, "Gorbachev Clears Way for German Unity, Dropping Objection to NATO Membership," *NYT*, July 17, 1990, p. A1.

224. "Excerpts From Kohl-Gorbachev News Conference," p. A8.

225. Schmemann, "Gorbachev Clears the Way for German Unity," p. A8.

226. Quoted in Thomas L. Friedman, "2 Germanies Vow To Retain Borders With The Poles," *NYT*, July 18, 1990, p. A6.

227. Yost, "France in the New Europe," p. 115.

228. Interview with the author, January 1992.

229. Gilbert Gorning, "The Contractual Settlement of the External Problems of German Unification," *Aussenpolitik* 42, no. 1 (1991), p. 11.

230. See Teltschik's account of this discussion in *329 Tage*, p. 337. In his testimony to the Senate Foreign Relations Committee as part of the ratification of the treaty, Robert Zoellick was vague on the linkage between the Bundeswehr limits, CFE and a Soviet troop withdrawal. He seemed to imply that the limit of 370,000 was tied to a CFE agreement, and the linkage to the Soviet troop withdrawal was politically binding but not legally binding. Committee on Foreign Relations, United States Senate, Hearing, *Treaty on the Final Settlement with Respect to Germany*, September 28, 1990 (Washington: Government Printing Office, 1991), pp. 32-6.

231. As reported by Teltschik in *329 Tage*, pp. 334-6.

232. "Das grosse historische Werk," *Der Spiegel*, September 17, 1990, pp. 19-20.

233. Ibid., pp. 19-20.

234. Thomas L. Friedman, "Four Allies Give Up Rights in Germany," *NYT*, September 13, 1990, p. A1. See also Goming, "The Contractual Settlement," pp. 10-11.

235. Serge Schmemann, "Agreement on Soviet Withdrawal Brings German Settlement Closer," *NYT*, September 11, 1990, p. A8.

236. Quoted by Udo Bergdoll, "Nach einem Lichtjahr am grossen Ziel angelangt," *SZ*, September 28, 1990.

237. Serge Schmemann, "A Historic Moment Slips By, Overshadowed," *NYT*, September 13, 1990, p. A6.

238. Bertram, "Ein Weltrekord der Diplomaten," p. 4.

239. Hugh Trevor-Roper, *History and Imagination* (Oxford: Oxford University Press, 1980), p. 2.

240. This has been one of the criticisms of the Baker style of decision making at the State Department. As a congressional source observed in regard to the Iraq crisis, "The very top [of the State Department] was focused on Eastern Europe, and Iraq didn't go up on their screen until July, when it was too late. [Assistant Secretary for Near Eastern and South Asian Affairs John H.] Kelly and others were sending danger signals." Quoted by Madison, "Baker's Inner Circle," p. 1737.

241. Maureen Dowd with Thomas L. Friedman, "Could Baker's Grip on Tiller Right Bush Campaign Drift," *NYT*, March 29, 1992, p. 14.

242. For a similar assessment, see Alexander Moens, "American diplomacy and German unification," *Survival* 33 (November/December 1991), pp. 531-45.

243. Quoted in Oberdorfer, *The Turn*, p. 438.

244. "Shevardnadze Addresses Panel," p. 20.

245. Teltschik, *329 Tage*, pp. 13-16.

246. As Arnulf Baring argues, however, this sort of reconciliation is unlikely for a long time. While France and Germany live at relative similar levels of economic development, the gap between Poland and Germany is far greater. Only after Germany is able to rebuild the eastern Länder will the preconditions exist for reconciliation with Poland. "The current German mentality allows us to say, We already have too much to do with the GDR. Now also Poland? They should look to themselves to see how they can progress." *Deutschland was nun?* (Berlin: Siedler Verlag, 1991), p. 103.

SELECT BIBLIOGRAPHY

Books and Publications

Asmus, Ronald. *German Perceptions of the United States on the Eve of Unification*. Santa Monica, Calif.: The Rand Corporation, 1991.

Baring, Arnulf. *Deutschland was nun?* Berlin: Siedler Verlag, 1991.

Barzini, Luigi. *The Europeans*. New York: Simon and Schuster, 1983.

Baumann, Eleanor, et al. *Der Fischer Weltalmanach Sonderband DDR*. Frankfurt: Fischer Taschenbuch Verlag, 1990.

Blechman, Barry M. and Cathleen Fisher, eds. *The Silent Partner: West Germany and Arms Control*. Cambridge, Mass.: Ballinger, 1988.

Calleo, David P. *Beyond American Hegemony: The Future of the Western Alliance*. New York: Basic Books, 1987.

DePorte, Anton. *Europe Between the Superpowers: The Enduring Balance*. New Haven: Yale University Press, 1979.

Freedman, Lawrence. *The Evolution of Nuclear Strategy*. New York: St. Martin's Press, 1989.

Gaddis, John Lewis. *Strategies of Containment: A Critical Appraisal of Postwar National Security Policy*. New York: Oxford University Press, 1982.

Gallis, Paul E. *The Unification of Germany: Background and Analysis of the Two-Plus-Four Talks*. Washington, D.C.: Congressional Research Service, 1990.

Gedmin, Jeffrey. *The Hidden Hand: Gorbachev and the Collapse of East Germany*. Washington, D.C.: The American Enterprise Institute, 1992.

Geipel, Gary, ed. *The Future of Germany*. Indianapolis, Ind.: The Hudson Institute, 1990.

Hacke, Christian. *Weltmacht wider Willen: Die Aussenpolitik der Bundesrepublik Deutschland*. Stuttgart: Klett Verlag, 1988.

Hanrieder, Wolfram. *Germany, America, Europe: Forty Years of German Foreign Policy.* New Haven: Yale University Press, 1989.

Horn, Gyula. *Freiheit die ich meine: Erinnerungen des ungarischen Aussenministers, der den Eisernen Vorhang öffnete.* Hamburg: Hoffmann und Campe, 1991.

Kaiser, Karl. *Deutschlands Vereinigung: Die internationale Aspekte.* Bergische Gladbach: Bastei Luebbe, 1991.

Klein, Hans. *Es begann im Kaukasus.* Berlin: Ullstein, 1991.

Laird, Robbin F. *The Soviets, Germany, and the New Europe.* Boulder, Colorado: Westview Press, 1991.

Larrabee, Stephen F., ed. *The Two German States and European Security.* New York: St. Martin's Press, 1989.

Menges, Constantine C. *The Future of Germany and the Atlantic Alliance.* Washington, D.C.: The American Enterprise Institute, 1991.

Ninkovitch, Frank A. *Germany and the United States: The Transformation of the German Question Since 1945.* Boston: Twayne, 1988.

Oberdorfer, Don. *The Turn: From the Cold War to a New Era—The United States and the Soviet Union, 1983-1990.* New York: Poseidon Press, 1991.

Pierre, Andrew. *Nuclear Politics: The British Experience with an Independent Strategic Force, 1939-1970.* London: Oxford University Press, 1972.

Pond, Elizabeth. *After the Wall.* New York: Priority Press, 1990.

Reilly, John, ed. *American Public Opinion and U.S. Foreign Policy 1991.* Chicago: The Chicago Council on Foreign Relations, 1991.

Schäuble, Wolfgang. *Der Vertrag: Wie ich über die deutsche Einheit verhandelte.* Stuttgart: Deutsche Verlags Anstalt, 1991.

Sodaro, Michael J. *Moscow, Germany and the West from Khrushchev to Gorbachev.* Ithaca, NY: Cornell University Press, 1990.

Stürmer, Michael. *Die Grenzen der Macht: Begegnung der Deutschen mit der Geschichte.* Berlin: Siedler Verlag, 1992.

Teltschik, Horst. *329 Tage: Innenansichten der Einigung.* Berlin: Siedler, 1991.

Trevor-Roper, Hugh. *History and Imagination.* Oxford: Oxford University Press, 1980.

Dissertations

Asmus, Ronald. "Bonn and East Berlin: The Politics of German Unity and Partition." Unpublished dissertation, Johns Hopkins University, 1991.

Selected Articles and Essays

Bertram, Christoph. "Ein Weltrekord der Diplomaten." *Die Zeit,* September 14, 1990, p. 4.

Bertram, Christoph. "Ausstieg eines Seiteneinsteigers." *Die Zeit,* December 21, 1990, p. 5.

"Bonner Schlüssel." *Der Spiegel,* no. 9 (February 26, 1990), pp. 20-1.

Buhl, Dieter. "Vom Paten zum Partner Bonns." *Die Zeit* (North American ed.), July 27, 1990, p. 5.

"Das grosse historische Werk." *Der Spiegel,* no. 38 (September 17, 1990), pp.18-21.

"Der Druck von unten wächst." *Der Spiegel,* no. 48 (November 27, 1989), pp. 14-8.

"Die Hoffnung heisst Germanija." *Der Spiegel,* no. 30 (July 23, 1990), pp. 16-26.

"Die Siegermächte warnen Bonn." *Der Spiegel,* no. 50 (December 11, 1989), pp. 16-9.

Diehl, Jackson and John Goshko. "4 Powers Stress 'Importance of Stability' Amid German Change." *Washington Post,* December 12, 1989.

"Ein Staatenbund? Ein Bundesstaat?" *Der Spiegel,* no. 48 (December 4, 1989), pp. 24-9.

"Eine Frage der Würde." *Der Spiegel,* no. 27 (July 2, 1990), pp. 18-22.

"Enormer Schaden für Moskau." *Der Spiegel,* no. 6 (February 5, 1990), pp. 42-58.

Fisher, Marc. "Kohl Proposes Broad Program for Reunification of Germany." *Washington Post,* November 29, 1989.

Friedman, Thomas and Michael R. Gordon. "Steps to German Unity: Bonn as a Power." *The New York Times,* February 16, 1990.

Garton Ash, Timothy. "Germany Unbound." *The New York Review of Books,* November 22, 1990.

Garton Ash, Timothy. "Mitteleuropa?" *Daedalus* 119, no. 1 (Winter 1990).

Gorning, Gilbert. "The Contractual Settlement of the External Problems of German Unification." *Aussenpolitik* 42 no. 1 (1991).

Gruneberg, Nina. "Der richtige Riecher: Helmut Kohl, Kanzler der Einheit." *Die Zeit* (North American ed.), October 5, 1990.

Haltzel, Michael H. "Amerikanische Einstellung zur deutschen Wiedervereinigung." *Europa Archiv,* no. 4 (1990), pp. 127-32.

Hoagland, Jim. "The End of the Special Relationship." *Washington Post,* December 7, 1989.

Hoagland, Jim. "Germans and French." *Washington Post,* December 14, 1989.

Hoffman, David. "Little-Known Aide Plays Major Role in Foreign Policy." *Washington Post,* October 21, 1991, p. A9.

Kaiser, Karl. "Germany's Unification." *Foreign Affairs, America and the World 1990/91* 70, no. 1 (Winter 1991).

Madison, Christopher. "Baker's Inner Circle." *National Journal,* July 13, 1991.

Moens, Alexander. "American diplomacy and German unification." *Survival* 33 (November/December 1991).

Newhouse, John. "The Diplomatic Round: Sweeping Change." *New Yorker,* August 27, 1990.

"Nicht den Buchhaltern überlassen." *Der Spiegel,* no. 20 (May 14, 1990), pp. 28-30.

Oberdorfer, Don. "Baker's Evolution at State." *Washington Post,* November 16, 1989, pp. A1, A43.

Oldenburg, Fred. "Sowjetische Deutschland-Politik nach der Oktober Revolution in der DDR." *Deutschland Archiv* 23 (January 1990).

Osborn, John E. "On the Reunification of Germany." *American Journal of International Law* 86, no. 2 (April 1992).

Schütze, Walter. "Frankreich angesicht der Deutschen Einheit." *Europa Archiv,* no. 4 (February 25, 1990).

Sloan, Stanley R. "The U.S. Role in a New World Order: Prospects for Bush's Global Vision." *CRS Report for Congress.* Washington, D.C.: Congressional Research Service, 1991.

Smith, Jeffrey R. "Power Shift Presages the Future Germany." *Washington Post,* July 6, 1990, p. A28.

Weilemann, Peter R. "The German Contribution Toward Overcoming the Division of Europe—Chancellor Helmut Kohl's 10 Points." *Aussenpolitik* 41, no. 1 (1990).

"Wendemarke der Geschichte?" *Der Spiegel,* no. 20 (May 14, 1990), pp. 18-27.

"Wir brauchen einen Vertrag." *Der Spiegel,* no. 17 (April 23, 1990), pp. 17-20.

"Wir haben dort mitzureden." *Der Spiegel,* no. 13 (March 26, 1990), pp. 18-21.

"Wir mussen es behutsam tun." *Der Spiegel,* no. 8 (February 19, 1990), pp. 16-8.

Yost, David. "France in the New Europe." *Foreign Affairs* 69, no. 5 (Winter 1990/91).

Speeches

Baker, James, III. "A New Europe, A New Atlanticism: Architecture for a New Era." *Current Policy* no. 1233. Washington, D.C.: Department of State, December 12, 1989.

Genscher, Hans-Dietrich. "German Unity Within the European Framework," delivered at the Tutzing Protestant Academy. *Statements and Speeches* 13, no. 2. New York: German Information Center, February 6, 1990.

"Joint Statement by Hans-Dietrich Genscher and Gerhard Stoltenberg on the Security Questions Concerning a Unified Germany," February 19, 1990. Press and Information Office of the Federal Government, Bonn. Bulletin no. 28.

Kohl, Helmut. "Ten Point Plan For German and European Unity." November 28, 1989. In Helmut Kohl, *Reden und Erklärungen zur Deutschland Politik*. Bonn: Press and Information Office of the Federal Government, February 1990.

Shevardnadze, Eduard. Speech before the CPSU Party Congress, July 3, 1990. "PRAVDA Carries 3 July Speech, Reports: Foreign Minister Shevardnadze," *Foreign Broadcast Information Service—Soviet Union,* July 6, 1990.

Shevardnadze, Eduard. Speech before the Foreign Affairs Committee of the Supreme Soviet. "Shevardnadze Addresses Panel on German Treaty." *Foreign Broadcast Information Service—Soviet Union,* September 21, 1990.

INDEX